TO BE A PRINCESS

TO BE A PRINCESS

Nimrod Liram

Copyright © Nimrod Liram
Jerusalem 2012/5772

All rights reserved. No part of this publication may be translated, reproduced, stored in a retrieval system or transmitted, in any form or by any means, electronic, mechanical, photocopying, recording or otherwise, without express written permission from the publishers.

Cover Design: Sylvie Liram
Typesetting: Irit Nachum

ISBN: 978-965-229-568-2

1 3 5 7 9 8 6 4 2

Gefen Publishing House Ltd.
6 Hatzvi Street
Jerusalem 94386, Israel
972-2-538-0247
orders@gefenpublishing.com

Gefen Books
11 Edison Place
Springfield, NJ 07081
516-593-1234
orders@gefenpublishing.com

www.gefenpublishing.com

Printed in Israel   *Send for our free catalogue*

Library of Congress Cataloging-in-Publication Data

Liram, Nimrod.
To be a princess / Nimrod Liram.
p. cm.
ISBN 978-965-229-568-2
I. Title.
PR9510.9.L57T6 2012 • 823'.92—dc23 • 2011042695

In Memory of:

James (Jim) Alley of Austin, Texas, USA
A close friend in crucial times, who departed this life too early.

Contents

Preface ix

To Be a Princess 1

Tel Shams 15

À Paris 25

Simon 39

Beirut, 1982: Theatre of the Absurd 55

Jean-Louis Meets His Match 69

Pendejo 82

Barracuda Reef 93

A Reasonable Person 108

The Maths Teacher 123

Preface

This collection contains ten short stories. It encompasses a forty-year span, between 1969 and 2009.

Eight of these are based on the author's own life experiences, or accounts as described by close protagonists. Sometimes they are a mixture of both. All stories are based on a solid kernel of true events. Their themes vary between high school romance, travel and misgivings about cultural differences, health care and issues of personal integrity and moral standards. They address various aspects of professional life in our highly complex real world.

The remaining two stories are autobiographic and documentary firsthand wartime tales, dealing with battlefield events referring to the 1973 and 1982 wars. These are written in the first person.

All stories are intended to provide a light but thought-provoking reading experience.

I would like to extend my heartfelt thanks to Prof. Nedda Strazhas, Prof. Leona Toker, Dr. Talia Trainin, Dr. Carol Goldfus and Mr. Mark Slater, for reading, commenting on and reviewing some or all of this work.

To Be a Princess
1969

Jimmy stood on the street corner by the large acacia tree at his usual bus stop. It was seven-thirty in the morning, and the bus was due in five minutes.

Looking up, Jimmy saw an elegantly dressed man and a young blonde girl walking towards him. The man wore a pair of white yachtsman's slacks, a blue sweater and brown penny loafers. His dark hair was brushed back, with a glossy hint of hair-cream shine. The young lady too was well dressed and kept her long hair in a bow. Her face resembled that of the older man, and Jimmy assumed that they were father and daughter. The gentleman approached Jimmy and asked, "Is this the bus stop for the American school?"

"It certainly is," replied Jimmy. "The bus will be here soon," he added.

The man and the girl both smiled, and the man said, "I'm Antonio Luis Sáenz. This is my daughter Gloria. We arrived from Buenos Aires last week and we are from the Argentine embassy. Gloria starts school today." Antonio's English was fluent, but with an obvious South American accent.

"Welcome," answered Jimmy. "My name is Jimmy Clarke and my family is from the US embassy. Well, my dad works there, anyway. I guess this street corner is becoming a favourite with the diplomatic corps."

The Argentine diplomat grinned and said, "Well observed, Mr. Clarke. Today, I'll wait for the bus with you both, but as of tomorrow, Gloria is your responsibility. You must see that she gets on the bus in the morning and gets off and walks home in the afternoon. Any problem with her," he winked humorously, "and you sound the foghorn."

Jimmy grinned back and replied, "Aye, aye, captain!"

Antonio stood at mock attention and answered, teasing, "It's *commander*, not full captain as yet. But you are quite right. I'm the new naval attaché."

The yellow bus arrived and Jimmy, feeling responsible, helped Gloria in before climbing up the stairs and into the bus himself. Antonio waved good-bye and disappeared around the corner as the bus turned.

Jimmy led the newcomer to his usual seat and sat down next to her. He briefly introduced her to the few familiar people in the surrounding seats, then turned to have a good look at her. Her hair was all shades of blonde, from auburn to platinum. She had green eyes and wore very light makeup. Physically, she resembled a young version of the French actress Catherine Deneuve. Her legs, exposed just above the knees, were slim and beautiful, and her shoes matched the purse she carried. She wore a stylish flowery printed dress and gave the impression of having stepped out of a fashion magazine for European debutantes. She was definitely overdressed compared with most American high school girls.

"Where did you transfer from?" Jimmy asked.

"I was at the American school in Zurich, Switzerland. That was my father's last posting. We were there up until a few weeks ago, then we went to Buenos Aires for a short home leave."

Her speech was precise, correct, slang-free and had no hint of a foreign accent.

"Are you a senior?" inquired Jimmy with curiosity.

Gloria smiled bashfully and said, "I'm a sophomore. I'll be sixteen next month."

"Well," said Jimmy, feeling suddenly proud, "I turned eighteen last January and will be graduating this summer." He looked at her, raised one eyebrow and said half seriously, "That makes me an old man."

They arrived at the school grounds and waited for the bus to pull up in the parking lot. Jimmy led Gloria gallantly to her first-period classroom and told her, "Shout if you need any help. It's your first day here, so you're allowed to." He turned around and hurried to his morning class.

By 3:15 p.m. they were both seated again in the yellow bus. Jimmy felt exhausted after his last period – gym with forty minutes of intensive basketball. Gloria looked as fresh as a rose, just as at their morning meeting. "Enjoyed your first day here?" Jimmy asked.

"Very much," was the answer. She carried some books in her arms and glowed with happiness. "I had a biology class with Dr. Gianetti and Russian with Mr. Vladimir. They are both excellent teachers."

"They are that, no doubt," said Jimmy. "But it's a pity that Gianetti isn't allowed to practice medicine in this country. His qualifications from Italy aren't recognized here, and he refuses to go through years of retraining. So he teaches biology in high school and at the university. They say that he is a first-class surgeon.

"Vladimir is a different story. He teaches Russian and maths, but really likes chess best. He runs the school chess club in the afternoons and often plays simultaneously against all fifteen club members. They never stand a chance. Not even Justin, who holds the city's junior chess championship."

Gloria drank in all this information. "Do you play chess?" she inquired.

"No, but Vladimir is my calculus teacher and he's brilliant. The greatest maths teacher in school. It's interesting that you chose Russian as a class. Why did you?"

Gloria thought for a short while and said, "Maybe I too will become a diplomat one day. If I do, Russian fluency would then be a great asset." They both laughed.

Soon they arrived at the street corner where they had boarded the bus early that morning. The driver pushed the door lever open and nodded to them. Jimmy helped Gloria down the metal stairs and onto the pavement. They walked along the avenue, and she took the path leading to the apartment building next to the one he lived in. "We're next-door neighbours, I guess," he said.

"Come by anytime," answered Gloria with a sweet smile, as she approached her glass-door entrance.

The following morning Gloria appeared at the bus stop wearing a pair of designer denims and a simple but fashionable T-shirt. Although casual, her appearance was sophisticated. She looked expensively dressed without being overly ornamental. Jimmy noticed the way she walked. European chic, he thought. His concept of American women was that they had almost invariably developed a cowboy's gait. Seldom could he find in them the grace and walking fluidity of French, Italian or Spanish women.

"Good morning, Gloria," Jimmy said with a big grin. "You look like a princess even in blue jeans!"

Gloria had worn her hair loose that morning. She shook her mane and said, "Thank you for your kind compliment, Jimmy. But actually, I am a princess." Jimmy was surprised, but his cosmopolitan upbringing kept him from waiving this statement as a product of a teenager's delusion. She did not appear to be nonsensical at all.

"A real princess?" he asked quizzically.

"I am a *Princesa de Castilla* – Spanish blue blood. This is not unusual. There are many Spanish nobility families living in Latin America. My family has kept their Spanish titles in South America for the past hundred years."

Jimmy had all kinds of questions, but his mind kept wandering to the realm of fairy tales with princesses, golden plates, towers, castle ramparts and frogs demanding to be kissed. Before he could collect his thoughts the bus stopped by the acacia tree; they got on and walked to their seat.

"You didn't tell me yesterday that your father is number one, the head of the US mission here," said Gloria.

Jimmy laughed. "You didn't tell me that you are a blue-blooded Spanish princess yesterday either, so I guess we're quits. What else did you find out about me in less than twenty-four hours?"

Gloria turned her head towards Jimmy and fired away: "You are one of just six seniors taking calculus. You took an achievement test in maths and did really well, enough to cause Mr. Vladimir to wag three tails in the faculty room. You're a track-team member and mile runner, holding the seventh place in the hall of fame for the school mile record. Texas State University School of Engineering in Austin has accepted you for the next academic year, with an honours scholarship. And last but not least, you like Brenda Sykes from the senior class. She is the only girl taking calculus."

Jimmy was stunned. "You just joined this school yesterday and I probably know less about what goes on in school than you do!"

Gloria pursed her lips sweetly. "Girls talk about everything."

"Busybody," he snorted, but without anger.

In the afternoon when they got off the school bus, Gloria

invited Jimmy up to see her house. He said that he needed to go home first, but could come by at five o'clock. A few minutes before 5:00 p.m. Jimmy brushed his cowlick into order, wiped the dust off his shoes and told his mother that he was off to see a schoolmate in the building next door and would be back home for supper. "Someone new in school?" his mother asked.

"Yes, from Argentina," Jimmy answered, and quickly closed the door before she could ask any more questions.

The doorman in Gloria's building buzzed Jimmy in through the front door, and a uniformed valet showed him in. Gloria's residence was beautiful, with luxurious wooden floor paneling and original paintings of caravels and frigates on the walls. In the living-room corner stood a metal plate with cross swords behind it and a Latin inscription at its base. It had symbols depicting body armour, some form of green fern and a pair of standing lions in inlaid coloured metalwork. Jimmy assumed that it was the family's coat of arms.

Gloria appeared in a white dress and asked him if he wanted a drink. Jimmy said that he did, and she offered a choice of whiskey, gin-tonic or dry martini. "I'll have a small whiskey," he answered. The valet instantly produced a tumbler with a generous measure of Cutty Sark, an ice bucket and a small plate of cashew nuts. "Ice, sir?" The valet handed him his drink, put the ice and cashews on a side table and left.

Jimmy and Gloria sat down and chatted for a little while. Her conversation was clever and witty, and he found himself enjoying her company. Although exposed to all sorts of diplomatic receptions due to his family's posting, Jimmy felt for the first time like the guest of honour in such upper-class surroundings. This was a far cry from an afternoon visit to a schoolmate, with soda and peanut-butter cookies. The drink had made him mildly light headed and relaxed. I could get used to this, he thought.

Half an hour later, the living room's heavy wooden door opened and Antonio Sáenz came in, briefcase in hand. Gloria ran up and hugged him, and Jimmy rose respectfully. Antonio sat down and chatted with the two while the valet brought his drink. He seemed pleased to see Jimmy and thanked him effusively for all his help to Gloria during her first days in school. "Don't mention it," said Jimmy. "Anyone would be delighted to help her out."

"Come and see us anytime, Jimmy," said the naval attaché, as Jimmy got up to leave.

Gloria saw him to the door and gave him a slight squeeze on the arm, holding the door open with her other hand. "Antonio likes you," she said. "He usually ignores my friends, even ambassadors' children. I haven't seen him sit down and have a whiskey with any of my school friends before."

Jimmy was just in time for supper at home. His father had already arrived back from work and was sitting by the dinner table reading, his half-moon spectacles perched on the tip of his nose. He looked up as Jimmy walked in. "What have you been up to, cowboy?"

"Making a dent in the Argentine naval attaché's duty-free whiskey stash," answered Jimmy.

Clarke senior chuckled. "So you met Commander Antonio?"

Jimmy reported the recent encounter, adding, "I'm surprised that you've already met Antonio Sáenz. He's been here for just over a week and seems to have met a fair number of people in a short time."

His father scratched his chin thoughtfully. "Sáenz is indeed a highly sociable fellow, but he is also a special case. In the Argentine navy, one's career may depend on the amount of blue blood in one's veins rather than on the amount of blue water one has crossed. He even managed to convince his command to send him to Switzerland, even though it has no sea outlet and no real navy to speak of. His naval career has been mostly diplomatic, while his mates spent far more time at sea. But make no mistake, he's known to have carried out some delicate negotiations for his government. We must therefore assume that he's held in high esteem. So far as I can tell, Antonio is a bright fellow with a razor-sharp reputation for troubleshooting. I'm glad that you've made his acquaintance."

Jimmy wondered why his father was being unusually talkative about Antonio, but decided not to comment on it.

One morning during the following week Gloria told Jimmy about a new film that had been the talk of the town, Roger Vadim's *Barbarella* starring Jane Fonda. The film had come out some months previously and she had read a review of it. Now it had arrived at the local movie theatre in the nearby shopping centre. "Let's go and see it tonight," Jimmy suggested. Gloria was surprised but delighted.

That evening they met at the movie theatre a few minutes before the show. Jimmy came directly from his track practice. Gloria arrived by taxi, looking lovely as usual and smelling even better. She turned down a keg of popcorn and settled for vanilla ice cream. They enjoyed the sexy sci-fi saga and chatted all the way home about the futuristic fashion carnival and the daring exposures of female flesh, which had been absent from US films until quite recently. Jimmy analysed it all as a "direct and influential derivative of the greatest sex revolution of the century: the contraceptive pill." Gloria found him bright and witty. He beamed at the compliment but thought himself somewhat verbose. He mused for a moment and said, "Well, no matter how hormonal Jane Fonda is, or how much breast and buttock she bares, she still walks like a cowboy."

Gloria laughed heartily. "I never thought that American men even noticed that!" Jimmy saw Gloria to her front door and waved a salute to the uniformed doorman. "See you tomorrow, Gloria. Same time, same place. Thanks for coming to the movies with me." She smiled, brushed a peck on his cheek and walked into the lobby.

As he watched her disappear into the building, Jimmy suddenly realised that Gloria was becoming infatuated with him. She was very good company and he found her interesting, even attractive. But his thoughts and dreams were about Brenda Sykes. Brenda was magic, although almost unapproachable. She was the unquestioned queen of the graduating class of 1969 and paid little attention to her male classmates. Her presence in their common maths class was cool and clever. She respected his achievements but was always distant. There was talk of a twenty-five-year-old college teacher whom she saw after school hours. Someone reported that on several occasions he had picked her up from school in a Volkswagen beetle. But he was never seen or discussed. Jimmy found it hard to think of Gloria as a substitute for Brenda in his heart. He could not fall in love with her.

Spending an hour or two with Gloria in the neighbouring building became habit. She invited him upstairs at least two or three times a week. Sometimes they drank a bit of her father's scotch. On other occasions he helped her out with homework, or just lay on the thick carpet in her room chatting and laughing. Although they had kissed a few times, Jimmy made it clear that they were not meant to be going steady. This disappointed Gloria but didn't seem to anger her to the point of quarreling or ending their friendship. Somehow, she appeared to accept it.

One day she was moody and told him that the world was unfair. Wesley from her biology class, she said, was madly in love with her. Although he was tall, smart and handsome, she wanted Jimmy. But Jimmy was not forthcoming, for a variety of reasons that were unclear even to him. Yet the next morning when they met on the bus, she was her sweet self again. Jimmy considered the situation and decided to lessen his contact with her in order not to frustrate her. But his plan didn't work, and he found himself spending time with her as usual.

That same week Mr. Vladimir had given their maths class an assignment to be carried out in pairs. To his surprise, Brenda chose him as her partner. They worked together for the rest of that day's maths class, and decided to carry on later in the library. After lunch, Jimmy had track practice and then met Brenda in the library. They worked quietly for a while and went for coffee. The senior lounge was empty. Popping a few coins into the coffee machine, they sat down to drink the foaming liquid in heat-proof plastic cups. Brenda complimented him for what she termed his "clear and creative mathematical thinking." Jimmy said that he did not quite understand what that meant, but if she liked his work, that was good enough for him. She laughed and suddenly asked, "Jimmy, why choose Texas State U? You could have gotten into any Ivy League college of your choice, and maybe even obtained a scholarship. Harry got a first-year scholarship to Princeton, and you scored higher than he."

"Two reasons," answered Jimmy. "One is that Texas has a first-class engineering school. The other is that we originally come from Austin. Before my dad was sequestered by the US Department of State and relocated to DC, we lived there. I applied to Texas State because many of my friends and most of my family are still in Austin, and the tuition would be much lower. But then they offered me the scholarship, and I couldn't say no to such an offer."

"Those are good reasons," said Brenda. She was going to Radcliffe and Jimmy couldn't tell whether her inquiry came out of curiosity, snobbishness or a genuine wish to know where he would be. He decided to find out.

"Why do you ask, Brenda?"

"Oh, I don't know," she replied atypically. "I hope they have a good track team in Austin." This was the first time that Brenda had acknowledged him at all. He was pleased, but at the same time realised that one swallow needn't mean spring.

That afternoon he rode the bus home with Gloria. She was very excited about life that particular week. Her sixteenth birthday was coming up, and she told Jimmy about the festivities that her father had planned for the occasion. Friends and family were arriving from Buenos Aires, and Antonio was planning a boat cocktail party with full white navy uniforms. Jimmy was pleased. That evening he bought her a copy of Hermann Hesse's *Siddhartha*, which he knew she hadn't read yet.

The following morning, he gave her the book under the acacia tree while they were waiting for the bus. He had asked the shop to gift wrap it in "sweet sixteen" shiny paper. Gloria was touched that he had gotten her something she had really wanted. On the way back home that afternoon, when they parted near her building, he realised that they hadn't spent any time together at her home for over a week. He thought that perhaps she was busy with the forthcoming birthday party and put it out of his mind.

Later that evening, Jimmy picked up the telephone and rang Gloria. He had an urge to talk to her without being able to pinpoint a specific reason. Antonio answered the call and told Jimmy that Gloria had gone shopping with her mother and would be in later. As Jimmy was saying good-bye, Antonio unexpectedly asked, "Have you got a moment now, Jimmy? Come up and see me at home if you can."

"Sure thing," said Jimmy. "I'll be there in a few minutes."

Antonio showed him into his study and poured generous measures of Cutty Sark into tumblers. He seemed relaxed and affable. After Jimmy declined a Cuban cigar, Antonio lit his own and said, "I need to reach some kind of understanding with you.

I am fond of you, and you're a bright and decent young man. But I must ask you not to come here or see Gloria outside of school."

Jimmy was surprised and annoyed. "Mr. Sáenz, I assure you that there was no ill meaning or objectionable conduct of any kind in my relation with her. We're just friends."

Antonio smiled back at him and said, "Not your fault at all, son. But we are Latin Americans, with traditions and habits that differ greatly from North Americans. We are Catholic and have a different lifestyle. Gloria is obviously infatuated with you. But she will be engaged to be married to a fine young man this week, on her sixteenth birthday. His name is José María, and our families have known each other for years. Gloria has known José since childhood and seems to like him. Officially, they will be engaged now and in all likelihood be married when Gloria turns eighteen and graduates high school. But for us, another male's presence can't be tolerated after a woman is engaged. You mustn't spend time with her alone, which is why we are having this conversation."

Jimmy thought for a moment and answered, "I guess I have to respect your request. I assure you that there will be no future conduct that might embarrass you or Gloria."

Antonio laughed heartily. "You don't understand a woman's heart, young man. Gloria is a stubborn young lady with a munificent combination of Latin passion and teenage hormones. Right now, she thinks that she is Barbarella. If she decides to have sex with you before you go away to university in America in four months time, there is nothing you or I can do to prevent it. This is an imminent risk, especially in this day and age of oral contraception. If you continue to spend time with her in her room, I may trust you to behave yourself, but I'm more worried about trusting her. So please, stay away from her. My family's reputation depends on it. If José María gets an idea that Gloria is spending time intimately with another post-pubescent male, the situation may become embarrassing. That is unfortunately the way we are."

Jimmy swallowed hard. He didn't want to annoy Antonio, but decided to ask anyway. "Can I ask just one question?" Antonio nodded in agreement.

"Does Gloria love this guy?"

The older man dropped ash from his cigar into the ashtray and relit it. He pondered for a little while and then said, "He's right for her. She is a princess. José will inherit a *conde*, the title of a count, from his father. He will complete a university degree at Valladolid in Spain this summer and go from there straight to the Argentine naval academy. When Gloria finishes high school, José will have already finished his officer's training. Then, they will be married. She told him about you. A hundred years ago, he would have challenged you to a duel. But as you see, Jimmy, we have come a long way since then, in particular for a society tangled up in too much religion, tradition, ego and testosterone." Antonio became pensive. "This is awkward for me, both because I like you, and also because your father is a high-ranking and respected member of the diplomatic corps."

Jimmy nodded in understanding, shook hands with Sáenz and walked home. He recalled what his dad had said some weeks ago about Sáenz and felt that he now understood it better.

Ambassador Clarke was sitting in the living room when Jimmy came in, looking at some paperwork with both feet propped up on the coffee table. Fortunately, his mom was not in evidence to see this assault on her standards of etiquette.

"What's up, son?" he asked. "You look like a ghost has seen you."

Jimmy sat down in the chair facing his father. "I've just been declared persona non grata by Commander Sáenz. His daughter will turn sixteen and be betrothed to some count, a naval academy cadet in Argentina. He politely asked me to get out of their way."

"Serves you right," said his father humorously. Then he added, "This city's diplomatic community seems to be full of romantic scandals these days."

Jimmy was suddenly curious. "How's that?"

"Well," answered Clarke senior, "the British embassy is in turmoil because the deputy ambassador's wife is pregnant. All would be otherwise delightful, but the responsible male, it appears, is the headmaster of the English school. The lady refuses to have termination due to religious creed. The headmaster cannot be tied to the post, since officially the school is a private one; he isn't a diplomat or an official envoy and doesn't have to abide by any state etiquette.

"In addition, the Israeli mission is boiling hot because one of their younger personnel is dating a pretty German cultural attaché whose father was a Waffen SS captain. When the ambassador asked him to break it off or get dismissed, the young colt threatened to make a public performance of it, marry the girl at the town hall in Munich and invite journalistic coverage from all over the world as witnesses. Their foreign office troubleshooter arrived from Jerusalem and is now trying to put the fire out and hush it all down."

The older Clarke put his paperwork down and looked at his son. He was enjoying all this. Having finished telling his son about all the scandals he added, "You needn't complain. You got a priceless lesson in risk management from a world-class master. I understand that it hasn't even cost a broken heart. Your troubles seem infinitely simpler in comparison, don't they, Jimmy?"

Tel Shams
1973

On October 5, 1973, I was assigned to Captain Benzion's command. We were based at the field artillery's main training facility. Not unusually, the training base was being swiftly transformed into operational regiments urgently put together. Officer cadets, trainee gun-commander candidates and training-base instructors filled manpower requirements. All these men were highly trained professionals. They happened to be taking part in one training programme or another at the time and belonged to the artillery school's manpower pool.

Military Intelligence HQ (headquarters) had forecasted a high state of alert and a strong possibility of a "battle day." In the Golan, this was not unusual. Hence, we were headed north in that direction on Friday, October 5, Yom Kippur eve. Benzion – or Benzi, as he was generally called – and I had not worked together prior to this particular alert, but I had heard about him and welcomed the idea of working with him at a real-time operational task. He was a newcomer to our unit and with a reputation for conquests, particularly among the female contingent of his previous post. I was interested and curious.

My usual specialty and charge at the training base was instructing tank terrain mobility and armoured-vehicle rescue.

But on Yom Kippur eve 1973, teams were rapidly being formed in any which way. Though I was assigned to Benzi's 155-mm howitzer self-propelled gun battery in an altogether different capacity, Benzi and I regarded my professional attributes as a bonus.

On October 5 the Golan defensive tank force was sparsely manned, with only Tank Brigade 188 and one extra regiment (82) borrowed from the Seventh Brigade. The infantry force consisted of Golani – a regular army infantry brigade – and Nahal Parachute Regiment 50 as reinforcement. The artillery umbrella counted approximately forty self-propelled pieces – mostly 155-mm howitzer guns, supplemented by a few self-propelled heavy 160-mm mortars.

In view of the possibility of a Syrian attack and a battle day, the Northern Command was trying to augment the regular army garrison by doubling the tank and gun power, but without resorting to a massive, multi-regimental reserve call-up. We were therefore bused to an emergency tank and armour storage depot at "Camp Philon" at the foot of the Golan, where we took over the stored artillery and vehicles belonging to a reserve regiment. Presumably, that particular regiment's staff would not need them for any immediate eventuality, since they were not called up. At least, IDF's (Israel Defense Forces) military intelligence worked along these assumptions.

Little did we know that within less than twenty-four hours, we would be outnumbered at a ratio of 1 to 45 and confronted with nearly one thousand charging Syrian tanks and many hundreds of Syrian artillery guns, all firing simultaneously.

During the third day of fighting, a British journalist crew sent in by the IDF spokesman unit joined Benzi's battery for a few hours. The reporter team consisted of a senior correspondent in his early thirties and a photographer who was quite a bit younger, in his early twenties. He seemed to be about my age and, unlike regular army soldiers, wore his hair long in the seventies' style. A very impressive set of cameras and lenses hung around his neck and more were stored inside his multi-pocket professional vest. For some reason, both journalists rode with us in the back of Benzi's vehicle.

We had been through hell those first few fighting days, whereas the British photographer who sat next to me looked clean and fresh. He seemed a little like a Baden-Powell scout, somewhat awkwardly out of his element. We were sitting on the vehicle's back bench and going through a bumpy ride when he asked me, "Do you think Israel will win this time?" I immediately answered, "Of course we will." Thinking that under the circumstances his question was somewhat naïve, if not stupid, I added, "I know what I'm doing here. I have to be here. But if I were you, I'd get the hell out of here as fast as I could." To his credit, he made no attempt to run away.

In retrospect, I can understand why during the first ten or twelve hours of the unexpected full-scale war that had befallen upon us we assessed the situation poorly. Ten to twenty hours to adjust to such a reality may be justified. But the encounter with the British journalists occurred over forty-eight hours into the war. By that time we had to have realised how grave and serious our position was. Israeli forces, including our own regiment, were evidently suffering massive losses.

There was no good reason at that point to think that we could win. Yet most of us kept going full force ahead because we understood no other way. Perhaps I was in fact more naïve than the British photographer.

Wartime events move fast, and a few days later, the brief delusional encounter with the journalists was long forgotten, lost in a mad and perilous sequence of fire, fight and dust, and mostly in the good fortune of staying alive.

On the afternoon of the seventh day of fighting, Benzi requested that I replace one of the tank drivers behind the steering sticks of the mobile artillery piece, a 155-mm French howitzer mounted on a modified Super Sherman tank. The poor fellow had been driving for nearly twenty hours straight and was dangerously tired. The symbiosis between commander and driver was compromised; a change of shift was urgently needed. I slid into the driver's seat.

The mobile battery moved downhill along a descending path formed by a partly asphalted, pitted old road. To our left rose a sloping hill and to our right a natural rock barrier, with a sharp drop into a wadi beyond it. The column of half-tracks, mobile artillery and jeeps rolled quickly down the road. Relatively high speed was determined by whatever maximum the Cummins diesel-powered Super Shermans could muster up on that particular stretch.

There was still quite a bit of functioning Syrian armour left scattered on the hillside, looking for prey. Benzi obviously wished to speed up. Having reached an asphalt-surfaced, closed road section with a sharp left bend, I noticed from my driver's hatch the gaping barrel bore of a T-55 Syrian tank pointing directly at us from behind a domed rock elevation on the mountain ridge to our left. The enemy tank was classically positioned to set the whole mobile column on fire within a minute or so. I had witnessed similar scenarios within the past days, and they were dreadful. Due to our high speed and lack of dispersing options to the left or the right, we appeared to be sitting ducks. Whatever decision making was possible, it needed to be made instantly. As I considered that the best option was to keep going, the gun commander's order came loud and clear through my earphones: "Step on it." We continued speeding along the trail, feeling that each one of our vehicles could, in a split second, turn into a hell-bound fire chariot on tracks.

But nothing happened. Immediately after the road bend we were all ordered to halt. I pulled myself out of the driver's hatch and yanked my field glasses out of their case. The tank whose gun had threatened us seconds ago was behind us, turret and profile exposed from where we now stood on the other side of the curve. The armoured vehicle was deserted, and on its turret's back were the scorched marks of a direct armour-piercing shell hit. This was invisible from where we had previously stood. The tank's gun appeared crooked and obsolete, like an empty threat. Benzi's vehicle came to a stop next to my hatch. He stuck his head out of the rolled-up nylon sheath window sewn into the vehicle's canvas canopy. His soiled face crinkled in a charred smile: "Scary, wasn't it?"

We kept driving along the same trail and deployed at the foot of Tel Shams. It was late Friday afternoon, in the middle of the Sukkot holiday (the Feast of Tabernacles). We had been fighting for only one week. But our routine deployment last Friday, on Yom Kippur eve, felt like an eternity away, and no signs of festivity were evident. Soon afterwards, battery target orders were given and we began firing.

I stayed near the crew that had needed my driving help and made an attempt to allocate my time to whatever was happening elsewhere within the battery. We were firing with moderate intensity, and I heard Benzi's radio set in the command vehicle report that our fire was aimed at helping a rescue operation underway. It later turned out that the operational aim was to bring in Lt. Col. Yossi Ben Hanan, who had been freshly appointed brigade CO (commanding officer) over whatever was by then left of Tank Brigade 188. The brigade's original CO was killed on the second day of the war, and Ben Hanan now lay injured somewhere on Tel Shams. This particular mission was on direct order from the divisional command. Our task was to back up the infantry mounted patrol rescue force that was sent to bring Ben Hanan in with accurate artillery fire, attempting to keep the Syrian army ground units from interfering with that action. A short-range 122-mm Syrian gun battery shelled the rescue area and contributed its share of difficulty in arriving at where the injured officer lay.

A half-track mounted infantry force was detailed to access the 122-mm gun battery from behind their lines and disable it at close range. That force had left the command post near us more or less when we began firing.

By that stage of the fighting, a week into the war, the Syrian army assault had been mostly halted. IDF armour was making attempts to penetrate the armistice line and punish the Syrian forces, who had taken heavy losses at the hand of the Israeli armoured garrison. These units were deployed when the hostility began, and were now backed up by effective reserve recruitment. But tactically, the situation was still fluid and could turn either way. Fresh Syrian forces had reorganised on Tel Shams. The dust had not settled yet. Ben Hanan's force was having difficulty trying a breakthrough to Sa Sa, in their attempt to open a route to Damascus. At that particular point in the entanglement the Tel Shams region happened to be a pivot in the battle aimed at shattering the second wave of Syrian attack. The odds could still turn in the enemy's favour.

Although no one said this out loud, our rescue mission seemed to gain first priority. This was reflected in the demands to increase firing tempo. We were now firing intensely. The gun crews were busy loading, unscrewing shell caps, preparing and tying up breech blast charges, breaking open fresh shell pallets and shooting at a mad rate. The 155-mm howitzers coughed out ammunition at a phenomenal speed. Empty charge cylinder cases, leftover blast bags and shell safety caps were scattered over the ground, contributing to the chaos.

Suddenly in the midst of the pandemonium, six Syrian 130-mm gun shells exploded one after the other in noisy succession about thirty metres behind the battery. These long-range, high-velocity shells have a typically evil shriek. Burning shrapnel, flying earth and broken basalt rock reached us; fortunately, no one was hurt. A quick look towards Mount Hermon showed clear skies – not a cloud. This meant that the Syrian artillery observation outposts on the high mountain had a clear view of us. We knew that clear skies and a long-range, six-gun battery hitting thirty metres short of our positions meant an accurate hit in less than a minute. We had learned the hard way that the Syrian artillery was both precise and effective. The present circumstances would prove it beyond doubt. We must move out immediately to an alternate firing position, I thought. I could hear Benzi's voice on the radio asking for permission to shift positions. "Negative. Keep firing from where you are" was the response I heard over the network loudspeaker.

Half a minute later, an ear-piercing explosion followed by the familiar shell whistles marked the beginning of inferno. Six shells landed almost at once inside the battery's perimeter. Explosion, tearing metal and screaming injured crews could be heard from just a few metres away. Over and above the burning live-shell hits, blast charges prepared for breech loading and leftover charge bags caught fire from the sizzling-hot shrapnel. Everything around me seemed torched and explosive. Blood-curdling screams for help were coming from the wounded, who were inaccessible to us due to the fire, dust and smoke. One man's voice kept screaming, "I'm dying, I'm dying…"

The columns of fire and smoke rose high and at that point, the radio loudspeakers called out: "Fold up. Move to alternate firing position." I climbed up the sloping Sherman's front end and slid into the driver's hatch, lowered the seat and started the engine.

Looking up, I saw the sky over the rectangular hatch opening glowing a bright red-orange. All this infernal fire around us had caused an impressive pyrotechnical effect, vividly lighting up the dark sky. Hell had never looked closer or more real than that sight from inside the tight iron pit of the Sherman's bowel. I prayed that live shells abandoned by the battery on the ground would not explode and turn our hasty retreat into a yet greater disaster. A direct hit on bare ammunition could cause an uncontrollable chain of explosion.

But the hellfire decided to spare some of us. We managed to form a sort of disorganised mobile row and quickly covered the few hundred metres to the alternate position. When we arrived, I got out of the hatch and asked the gun commander to place his driver back on duty. I was needed elsewhere and found my own half-track, originally detailed for rescue and recovery.

I quickly drove to where the medical team was taking care of the injured. The extent of the disaster became obvious. The dead lay on the ground covered with army-issue blankets. The heavy, acrid smell of burning flesh choked my throat and nostrils. The medics worked hard. I asked who had been killed, and one of them rattled off names. This was hard to swallow. Two of my own team members lay injured, with severe shrapnel hits in their legs. They were laid on stretchers, awaiting evacuation by air. The damaged vehicles bore silent testimony to the devastating artillery damage. The freshly shelled metal had shiny exposed alloy scars sheared and mangled by shrapnel. The metal told the story of its human tissue equivalent. Unlike a bullet injury that usually makes a clean hole, flying shrapnel tears, severs and deforms human muscle, blood vessels and bone. All this lay in plain sight before me.

The medical team was busy stopping the bleeding by tourniquet application, inserting intravenous infusions, immobilizing broken limbs, injecting morphine, tying the wounded to stretchers and evacuating them by air and land. Bits of ammunition and scorched vegetation were still smouldering around the targeted area. The rescue helicopter with the airborne medical crew and the wounded Ben Hanan, rescued along with his tank driver, flew over our heads on the way to Rambam hospital in Haifa. Soldiers less severely wounded were transported by land to the Safed hospital. There was little more that I could do to help, other than lift stretchers into rescue vehicles.

Once evacuation of the injured had ended and the medical crews had left, I suddenly found myself alone by the half-track. The engine still purred, and I drove straight to where Benzi's command vehicle stood. It was already late evening. Ben Hanan's rescue operation had ended, and the patrol that had carried it out returned to the brigade's command post. The basic tenet of the IDF code, not to leave a wounded soldier on enemy ground, had been obeyed. Its price tag had been unbearably high this time.

The infantry force sent out to disable the 122-mm guns had also returned, but reported an incomplete mission. The battery they were sent to destroy turned out to be dummy guns placed by the Syrians as decoy aimed to confuse our scouts.

We gathered the scattered battery crews who still roamed in the vicinity of the targeted area, collecting leftover equipment and materials. Benzi ordered single-file movement on tracks to where he wanted us to spend whatever was left of that lethal night. The atmosphere was heavy. Shock, loss and fear struck us all at once and we suddenly understood where we were. Confronting the violent death of those closest to us was different from acknowledging the death of those belonging to other units, or even those from our sister battery hit six days earlier. The event gave rise to a different kind of horror, one too close to home. Although some of our men had suffered injury prior to the Tel Shams night, none had been fatal. Now we could see the signs of despair and fear taking their toll. No one dared to ask "Who will be next" out loud, but the question prevailed on everyone's mind.

Shelling from enemy artillery had that kind of Russian-roulette effect. Every tree branch moving in the wind, or rustling cloth in the darkness seemed like a lurking enemy. Every distant whistle sounded like a nearby shell explosion.

I thought about the patrol soldiers who had passed us on the way to the brigade's HQ a short while ago. They seemed happier and felt better than we did. Even the infantry force that had not destroyed a real battery because it found only dummy guns showed no signs of the distress that had taken hold of our battery.

Strange, I thought. All three forces were involved in exactly the same mission. In theory, the risk was evenly distributed three ways. Perhaps the odds were even slightly worse for the rescue patrol which moved on enemy ground. The air-force rescue helicopter and its medical team ran a great risk as well. All participating units had been through a lot during those battle days and suffered casualties. Now it was our turn to lick our wounds.

Benzi spread his sleeping bag next to mine on the rock bed where we had chosen to spend the night. We had tried unsuccessfully to find a ditch, or even a shallow ground dimple that could serve us as shelter. "We could easily be shelled here too," Benzi said optimistically before rolling into his sleeping bag and falling asleep.

À Paris
1974

Tarzan's dark blue boiler suit was in sore need of washing. Mike and Rudi had pointed this out night after night, whenever they shared a late-evening shift with him at the Elf petrol filling station by the Place Stalingrad. The cover-all garment stank of petrol, motor oil, perspiration and cigarette smoke. During the late shift, Tarzan always looked sweaty, pallid and scarecrow-like in his oversized overalls. He had barely been able to manage the daytime shift; working nights appeared to be intolerably tiresome for him and he seemed completely out of his element. His eyes looked unusually large, giving him an owlish look behind the bottle-bottom spectacles without which he was blind as a bat. Yet when evening came, traffic through Place Stalingrad towards Place Pigalle and Montmartre thickened, with Parisians and tourists herding down Boulevard de la Chapelle into the red-light district and entertainment quarter. Thus, Monsieur le Pompiste (petrol pumper), the filling-station owner, needed a helping hand to cover for Tarzan, especially on weekends from ten o'clock at night to two o'clock in the morning.

Mike and Rudi were neighbours. They lived up Avenue Secrétan, by Place Stalingrad. They had rented a flat in an old walk-up seven-storey building together with Jaime, their university mate. All three had decided to travel and attend a basic course in French at the Alliance Française in Paris. Study sessions occupied their weekday afternoons. When not at school, they all looked for odd jobs to earn a few francs, as life in Paris was costly. Jaime managed to secure steady work in a Rue Passy boutique, near the Étoile.

One evening when tanking up their old VW beetle for a super busy night, Mike and Rudi had waited in line for nearly fifteen minutes. They immediately spotted an opportunity and inquired about a job at the filling station, approaching Monsieur le Pompiste. The boys were hired on the spot, in spite of the severe difficulty in deciphering the Pompiste's heavy Normandy accent. His speech rumbled with a moist guttural sound that came from the depth of a chronic lung and throat condition. His words were spoken through a cloud of smoke from an ever-present Gitanes Maïs that was stuck in his lips. He had told the enterprising youngsters that their pay would be four francs an hour. But whatever tips all staff pooled would be equally shared three ways with Tarzan at the end of the night. That seemed fair, but Monsieur le Pompiste and Tarzan were soon surprised and delighted. Mike and Rudi quickly and efficiently quadrupled the station's car fueling intake during the busy weekend night hours. The improved revenue more than doubled Tarzan's average tip volume, which made him smile constantly.

Around two o'clock in the morning, the filling station closed down. Tarzan habitually counted his loot and then walked home. Monsieur le Pompiste usually climbed up the iron staircase leading to his tiny, lonely studio on the floor above his fuel pumps. Occasionally, he got into his Renault 12 after work and roared off at great speed, to return late the following morning.

Jaime, Mike and Rudi attended class with a small group of European students. Their class consisted of Jean and Lily, a quiet young Swiss couple; Johan, an athletic German teacher; Montserrat, a beautiful entertainment manager from Barcelona; and Jenni and Dia, two smiling Dutch girls who went to university in Amsterdam. The Dutch girls were constantly provoked by Johan, who was an avid football fan. Germany and Holland had competed at the world cup finals that July, and sport-inspired animosity caused heavy badgering within the otherwise placid group.

The male trio complemented the pan-European human mosaic, holding the group socially alive and culturally active after school hours. Most evenings, they piled up into the VW beetle and drove to someone's house for dinner. In the summer of 1974 the Parisian gendarmes still showed little objection to seven or eight smiling young faces all squashed into a Volkswagen with foreign number plates. On their way from the Alliance Française they usually picked up meat at the Boucherie Bernard, vegetables at the open-air market on Avenue Secrétan and *vin ordinaire* for one franc a litre at the nearby *épicerie*. The boys' flat had no refrigerator; hence food bought had to be prepared and eaten that same night. Their simple abode hosted many a jovial dinner party, with wine and bottled Normandy cider flowing like water, and song and dance continuing into the small hours of the morning.

As Mike and Rudi were constantly seeking to earn a few more francs, Jaime came up with an attractive offer for them. Marie-France, the young boutique manager who employed him at Rue Passy, required someone who could come in daily during the lunch hour, clean the shop up and do odd maintenance jobs on demand. The offer increased their earnings, so Mike and Rudi shared the new responsibility and turned up at the boutique daily before the staff went out for their lunch break. Marie-France would show them light bulbs that needed changing in the display, fixtures that required repair and boxes that had to be packed, unpacked or thrown away. But their main task was to take the vacuum cleaner for a long three-storey dance, to look after the store's all-level wall-to-wall carpeting. That had been Marie-France's fetish and she insisted on spotless and dustless floors.

Marie-France usually returned at around three o'clock slightly tipsy from her lunch break, parking her small Solex moped on the pavement in front of the shop's window display. After her carpet inspection, she sat with them for a few minutes and sipped an espresso that was always ordered from the nearby café. They got paid cash in hand for their labour, and left Rue Passy together with Jaime for their French class. Marie-France was thrilled to have three male, Francophile, foreign university students working in her boutique that summer. She seemed friendly, and tried always to look her best, show off her proficiency in English and yet retain her slightly bitchy "boss" stance. All three boys found this whole arrangement very sexy.

One evening after their French lesson, it was unanimously decided to have dinner at Montserrat's apartment on Rue Diderot near Métro Pantin. They got into the VW – Mike driving, Jenni sitting on Rudi's lap in the front seat, four people packed into the back seat like sardines in a can and slim Jaime cooped up with miniature Dia in the beetle's "tub" behind the back seat. The car screeched and groaned but managed to get them to their destination.

They bought veal steak on the way, but had not decided about an entrée for their menu. Someone suggested escargot, and Montserrat quickly pointed out that the best snails she had ever seen were at the Cimetière Parisien de Pantin-Bobigny right across the street from her apartment building. Mike seemed fascinated by this gourmet suggestion. Enthusiastically, he got hold of Montserrat's hand and walked her to the cemetery gate. Although it was already getting dark, she went along with his drive. But once they entered the rows of tombstones, dusk was setting in and she flinched and dug her fingernails deep into Mike's forearm. "Let's get out of here," she cried, with pallid fear that could not be argued with. No snail-dish promise could budge her one step further.

Thus the initiative for that particularly interesting culinary adventure was aborted in favour of a lump of *pâté de foie gras* that was on sale at the *épicerie* where they bought the table wine.

Montserrat's Spanish roommates were all at home. Mike, Jaime and Rudi took charge of cooking *escalope de veau au citron* for fifteen; dinner was served past 11:00 p.m. and ended after midnight. The liver pâté was followed by veal, then salad *vert*, and was washed down with litres of *vin ordinaire*. After eating, Spanish guitars came out, and Montserrat with her roommates spontaneously produced a fiery flamenco performance. Brandy and coffee were poured, and the party split up after 3:00 a.m.

As everyone was too drunk to drive, the three boys walked the Dutch girls to their home and arrived at Avenue Secrétan by 5:00 a.m. They climbed all the way up the creaking wooden staircase to the seventh floor, where two flats occupied the top of the building: their own, and a twin one inhabited by two aristocratic café-au-lait sisters from Abidjan who attended university in Paris. The boys showered in turns and prepared to go to sleep when their doorbell rang angrily.

Monsieur Durant, their sixth-floor neighbour, stood at the threshold wearing a tasseled sleeping cap and a pair of long pajamas. His face wore an extremely irritated expression and in his anger he had difficulty making himself understood. Finally, he managed to convey his wish:

"Écoutez," he said, "I am an *infirmier* in the hospital. I work at night and come home at five in the morning. When I go to sleep, you make pee-pee and use the toilet flush. But my bed is next to where the building's sewage pipes run through the walls and they are loose, old and rusty. Every time you pull the flush handle, the water makes the pipes clank, shudder and rattle noisily past by my head, and I wake up. Now I cannot sleep!"

The three boys looked at each other in amazement. "What can we do to help you?" asked Jaime.

"Don't use the toilet before noon. That way, I won't wake up." This was easily settled and immediately agreed upon. Once Mr. Durant had accomplished his mission, the anger receded from his eyes and he walked downstairs, cap and tassel flapping. When the door closed behind him, Rudi thoughtfully suggested that they would be best served buying three bedpans, just in order to show support and solidarity with Paris's hospital working staff.

When they woke up past midday, Mike and Rudi took the Métro to Pantin station in order to retrieve the VW which had been left by Montserrat's flat.

Remembering the previous night's dinner party Rudi recalled, "I noticed that you were hovering all over Montserrat last night."

"After the flamenco performance, she became relaxed and quite amorous," Mike responded. "She had had a few glasses of her own brew of sangria plus a couple of brandies. She became mellow and sexy and said that she knew I fancied her. All this happened in French with a Barcelona accent and was wonderfully aphrodisiac. But then she sobered up a bit, recoiled and told me that she was Catholic and would only give herself to the man who marries her."

"Huge waste," said Rudi. "But she still makes a hell of a sangria."

Both agreeing on the waste and sangria scores, they got into the beetle and drove to Marie-France's boutique and their rendezvous with a vacuum cleaner.

At the end of their day's chores, Rudi teased Marie-France

about the intimate personal attachment that he had developed with her vacuum cleaner. "*L'aspirateur s'apelle Eric*, the vacuum cleaner is called Eric. We are now soul mates," he joked, hugging the vacuum cleaner's wide, accordion-like intake hose.

Marie-France found this idea amusing. "I've been meaning to tell you boys," she mentioned, "that in the middle of August I am going on vacation to Cannes with some friends. We rented a seven-room beach villa for two weeks and it has plenty of spare room. The three of you are welcome to drive down and spend a few days with us if you like." The boys discussed this as an attractive option for the second half of August.

The language course at the Alliance Française ended on the last day of July. They all took their exams, got their certificates and partied, first with their teachers and later by themselves until the early hours of the morning. Their group was splitting up, with Johan and Montserrat going back by train to their home countries the following day. The Swiss couple lived in Paris anyway, and both Dutch girls wished to stay on in town for another few days. They needed a place to sleep, and were offered space in the boys' flat. The girls accepted the offer, laying their backpacks and rolled sleeping bags on the living-room floor.

There were farewells and tears, but the three boys had another month's lease for their flat on Avenue Secrétan and were in no hurry to end their course of French culture just because school was over. They felt that the education that they had come for was yet incomplete and needed practice to reach perfection.

On Saturday Mike and Rudi were on duty at the petrol station and both hankered after adventure. Tarzan went home just after 2:00 a.m. and Monsieur le Pompiste, who had been fuelling his own thirst with Pastis all night, seemed to want them to come along with him in his car. His breath was charged with alcohol fumes and they feared that it could quite easily ignite by the glowing end of his Gitanes. The beetle was left parked at the filling station, and against their better judgment the two of them got into his Renault. Le Pompiste drove at a hideous speed, screeching around corners and skidding race-driver fashion on the cobblestoned roads through obscure *arrondisments*.

He pulled up in front of what looked like a bar. When they entered the room, all present seemed hostile and uninviting. But as soon as it became evident that the two strangers were Monsieur le Pompiste's guests, the animosity vanished. They were served drinks at the bar, yet any attempt to pay was declined. Everybody had something in common, but Mike and Rudi couldn't quite figure out what. Obviously, this was an establishment that hosted people who knew each other well. Apparently, many of them came from Rouen, Pompiste's hometown. More drink and food kept coming from the kitchen to the tables, and a saxophone-and-harmonica duo played a melancholy jazz tune from a corner in the salon. Taking Rudi and Mike to such an exclusive milieu was probably Monsieur le Pompiste's way of thanking them.

The event flowed on naturally almost until breakfast, by which time everyone was friendly and talkative, familiar and quite drunk. Their host, who had been drinking heavily all night, was almost unconscious, so Mike got behind the Renault's wheel. He had no idea where he was, but followed the signs for Boulevard Périphérique; from there he could quickly navigate to Place Stalingrad. They deposited their employer in his bedroom and climbed to their seventh-floor home. "Now that we met his ex-Normand exile colony I understand where he disappears some nights," Rudi commented. "It's easy to guess why he only returns in midmorning."

Upon reaching their floor, the cardboard-thin walls could hardly mask the unmistakable sounds of enthusiastic lovemaking from the Ivory-Coast girls' apartment next door. "African Genesis," muttered Mike, recalling the title of a pseudo-anthropological book he had read a while ago.

They sidestepped the inert figures of Jenni and Dia, sleeping on thin foam-rubber mattresses in the hallway, and climbed into their beds. "Don't flush the toilet!" Rudi warned Mike before falling asleep.

When Rudi woke up it was already past midday. Mike was fast asleep and Jenni was up and about, getting ready to go downstairs. The open-air market at the Marché Secrétan was open for business, so they decided to go and shop for fresh food. As they walked down the staircase, Jenni said that she fancied a coffee before they began shopping. The café at the street corner was open, and Rudi stood by the bar and ordered two café grand crème. The lad behind the bar operated the shiny, pressure-gauged coffee machine with speed and efficiency, promptly producing two frothing white coffees for them. Rudi slid one mug towards Jenni and placed his foot on the lower bar railing, holding the mug and sipping his coffee. She gave him the dirtiest look in Paris that day and said, "Do you think that you are in a stinky pub? Aren't you going to invite me to sit down?" He had hardly expected that reaction. Arguing with her seemed futile so he apologised and took both coffees to a sitting stall. No reason to offend anyone, he thought.

When they were through drinking, it was time to peruse the fresh food stalls, enjoying the colours and odours as well as the never-ending variety of country cheeses and smoked sausages on cleverly arranged, artful displays. "A true feast for the senses," said Rudi when they ascended back up the staircase to the flat. Jenni seemed to have overcome her irate spell and smiled sweetly. As they climbed upstairs with their shopping bags, the two African sister students from Abidjan walked downstairs. Rudi beamed at his neighbours and gave them each a hug. Jenni, who had been a guest in their flat for just a few days, mentioned with a disapproving scowl that "they have sex all the time, and seem to have different men every day."

He thought that Jenni had no business begrudging anyone enjoying life any way they wished, but remembered the café incident. Maybe she's having a bad day, he thought, and decided to keep quiet. She and Dia were leaving for Amsterdam that evening. They were dear to him and he saw no good reason to bicker now, or even disagree over anything.

Before setting out to go to work at the petrol station, they drove Jenni and Dia to the Gare du Nord train station not far from their flat, where they took the train to Holland. Their French study group had thus completely disintegrated. There was a distinctive feeling that part of the Parisian episode had come to its closure when the two backpacking Dutch girls in blue denims melted into the crowd on the way to the Amsterdam-bound platform.

While Mike and Rudi were bidding farewell to the last of their French study group, Jaime was tied up in a sizzling-hot relationship with a young Parisian lady who had shopped for a T-shirt at the boutique. She had asked for his assistance in and out of the changing room multiple times, until he finally ended up escorting her home with six different T-shirts. Since that night, Jaime was scarcely seen at the flat in Avenue Secrétan. He was in love and having the time of his life. Obviously, under the circumstances it was fair to assume that he would not be traveling to Cannes with them or accepting Marie-France's invitation.

After the middle of August, Mike and Rudi set out to drive to the Riviera. They took back roads, both in order to see the countryside and to avoid toll roads. Arriving at Cannes a couple of days later, they searched for the café where Marie-France had told them that the villa's owners worked. After finding the place, they got directions for the beach house, a few kilometers from the town. They found Marie-France and her friends having breakfast on the front balcony. The beach was just a few metres away, and the location beautiful. Marie-France seemed surprised to see them. She cried out "I don't believe it!" when the VW beetle rolled into the driveway. She hadn't quite thought that they would come, despite their promise.

The major shortcoming was that instead of a seven-room house, the owners had ended up letting the Parisians a much smaller villa. It only had two bedrooms and a large living room that opened into a front balcony. One bedroom was occupied by a young married couple, a seaman and his wife. The second bedroom was taken by a taciturn twenty-six-year-old Parisian economics graduate who insisted on having the room for himself on the sole merit of holding a university degree. He smoked a pipe and kept a snobbish distance from everyone else. Marie-France and three teenage boys aged fourteen to seventeen shared the living room and slept on folding cots. There had obviously been some tension around this subject and it was somewhat aggravated by the new arrivals. Mike and Rudi quickly assessed the situation and decided that camping in their sleeping bags on the front balcony was an adequate solution. They found a cool, shaded corner by the barbecue stand and told Marie-France that they were fine and she should put her mind at ease.

They spent the rest of that day at the beach, swimming and playing ball on the sand. There was but one small apartment block sharing the same secluded beach stretch, with several German tourists sunbathing and swimming. Occasionally, the local gendarmes turned up in a small Jeep and warned all visitors that swimming in the nude was forbidden. They didn't, however, take any measures to enforce this, instead choosing to disappear behind the sand dune and peep through field glasses at topless girls.

At night, Mike had a good charcoal fire going in the barbecue grill and roasted sausages. Rudi made some potato chips and everyone sat on the balcony and enjoyed the meal and wine. Later, when all were tired and sleepy, Marie-France and the young teenagers opened cots and spread them through the living room. They left the sliding doors to the balcony open to let in air. Mike and Rudi laid down ground mattresses and their sleeping bags on the balcony floor.

A short while after they turned the lights out, Marie-France got out of her cot and walked a few steps to where Mike and Rudi lay. She wore nothing but a minimal negligee and got into Rudi's sleeping bag, half closing the bag's zip after her. There was laughter and then some whispering, but a few short moments later she got out of the sleeping bag and went back to her cot.

When they woke up in the morning, Mike and Rudi walked over to the waterfront for a cool swim. Mike asked, "What was Marie-France on about with you last night?"

Rudi laughed. "What does a lady want with anyone, when she gets into his sleeping bag at night wearing next to nothing and no underwear?"

"I understand," said Mike. "But I know that you fancied her all the way from Paris. You would have personally and gladly changed places any day with the saddle of her moped. Nevertheless, after getting into your sleeping bag she seemed to change her mind and went back to her own bed."

Rudi agreed that was truly what had happened and added, "I told her that the choice of surroundings for intimacy was a little too indiscreet. I would have been much happier without three wakeful and curious teenagers as well as you in your sleeping bag right next to us; I might have found the whole arrangement far more enticing without the extra audience."

Mike pondered over this for a moment and said with concern, "That's food for thought. I hope that she took no offense."

"Nothing like that," replied Rudi. "She took an altogether pragmatic stance over it and said that she would effectively discuss the intimacy constraint with the pipe-smoking economist today and solve the rooming problem."

Mike seemed satisfied by this account and summed up, "Then it's a clear case of '*tu veux ou tu veux pas.*'"

They spent a few gorgeous days in Cannes and then drove to Paris, taking the motorway to save time. August 31 was only a few days away, and it was time to tie up loose ends, pack up, bid farewell and vacate the Avenue Secrétan flat. They called Jaime at the boutique and told him when they would be back. He came by with his girlfriend to help pack their worldly belongings. The two had been living at her home for the past couple of weeks and Jaime had hardly been to the flat at Avenue Secrétan. Amazingly, all their gear managed to fit easily into the VW. "It seems that we've collected mostly memories, not belongings," Rudi reflected.

Then, they went by to bid Tarzan and Monsieur le Pompiste farewell. The Normand was sober and pleasant, and gave them a bottle of Pastis Pernod as a parting present. Tarzan seemed sallow and sad, and made them promise to come back the following summer.

Between the three of them they could spare over a thousand francs, the money coming mostly from their rental deposit which had been reimbursed. They decided to spend the money at La Tour d'Argent. They borrowed used jackets and ties from the boutique and somehow managed to order a table on short notice at the famous restaurant. This was their personal Paris farewell party. After reaching an uneasy agreement over the wine with a quarrelsome sommelier, they ordered food and waited in the beautiful hall. Mike inquired, "Jaime, will you be crossing the channel back with us tomorrow morning, or are you staying on in Paris?"

Jaime said, "We're due at university in early October and today is just August 31. I suppose that I could stay here another few weeks and catch up with you two towards the end of September. I have some decision-making issues to resolve here before that. What are the two of you planning?"

Mike answered, "We'll be driving from the restaurant and catching the Dover ferry from Calais past midnight. The boat arrives in Dover at the crack of dawn. We have a hop-picking job lined up on a farm in a small village near Maidstone in Kent, about an hour's drive from the ferry. I'm told that the work is hard, but pays rather well. I spoke to the governor yesterday. He is used to employing students at this time of the year and needs as many workers as he can get for the hop-harvest season. We're expected at the farm early in the morning on September 1."

Simon
1979

The yoke was heavy and dug deeply into Simon's shoulders, biting a painful imprint on his skin where the harness lay. The load of dark grapes overflowed the wooden buckets swinging from the sturdy wooden frame. His tall figure stooped under the burden as he climbed up the mountain slope. It was dusk, with a September sun painting the vineyard landscape a soft purple-pink.

Bending from the knees, Simon carefully lowered the buckets, emptying their contents into a bin. He removed his T-shirt and massaged his aching shoulders, first in agony and then in relief. Perspiration beaded his brow, mixing with dust from the brown mountain soil to create a camouflage pattern on his face. He bent down towards his foot and removed a small lump of hardened earth, which had lodged itself painfully between the shoe and his bare foot. His labour for the day over, he sighed, thinking that his employer was pushing him to the limits of his physical strength.

The grape-harvesting job had been acquired by fortuitous accident at the marketplace in the neighbouring small town. A fortnight earlier, Panos, his employer, had driven into the open-air market in a small Peugeot truck loaded with crated grapes. He had noticed the tall, bearded youth with a knapsack on his back standing aimlessly among the fruit stands. The Greek farmer had motioned Simon to come and help him off-load the Peugeot, giving him a large bunch of grapes and one hundred drachmae for his effort once the task had been completed. As Simon had prepared to leave, shouldering his backpack and waving good-bye, Panos had had a brilliant idea. In his mind's eye, he had seen this powerful, if somewhat slim foreigner saddled with a yoke and two buckets, working for him in the vineyard. This lad is as strong and wiry as a mule, he had thought. I could do with his help for the remainder of the harvest.

The first and obvious hurdle was how to convey the offer to his prospective employee. Panos could speak no foreign language. Simon was waving good-bye and had almost melted into the marketplace crowd to disappear forever. In order to attract his attention, the Greek took a wad of drachma notes out of his pocket and waved it in the air in front of the youth's surprised face. The sound of rustling currency served its purpose, forestalling Simon's departure. Then, he motioned to the seat next to the driver in the front cabin of the truck. "*Arbeit*" (German for *work*), he called, waving the money again, using the only foreign word he could find to indicate that he wished to engage Simon in paid labour. The young man shrugged his shoulders and thought, Why not?

He found adequate space for himself and the rucksack and folded his long frame into the front seat of the Peugeot. As the Greek started coaxing the column gearshift to engage, Simon said to him, offering his hand for a handshake, "I am Simon. English, not Deutsch!" Panos's eyes brightened and he repeated emphatically, "Ingliss!" driving off at once, before the young fellow could change his mind. He could not believe his good fortune.

For Simon, the work offer meant that he could extend his holiday in the Ionic sun. He had been a little too carefree with the drachmae, drinking ouzo and ferry-hopping from one lovely island to another. Finally, he had made it back to the mainland, and had little choice but to hitchhike his way back home. His money had all but run out and would cover only minimal needs and hardly any travel fare.

Panos felt that since the initial recruitment had been successful, he must now try to make his new subordinate feel at ease. Therefore, he made an attempt at some sort of conversation. This was no easy task given the language gap. He pointed his finger at Simon and asked, "Engineers?" Simon thought that Panos may be trying to find out whom he had hired, exhausting the extent of his English vocabulary in the attempt. He answered, "I am a psychiatric nurse," immediately realising the futility of his verbal effort. After a blank look from Panos, he thought for a few moments of an adequate mime description of his qualifications. He pointed his index finger to his temple and made twisting motions, as if to denote "mad." While doing so he said "doctor," assuming that the Greek would be acquainted with this international word. This seemed to work to a satisfactory level. Indeed, the farmer had gathered a general impression that he had unknowingly hired some sort of an English mental-health professional.

But in truth, Panos was impressed with the young man's strength, rather than the added bonus of his professional qualifications. Harvesting grapes on his land required great physical strength and endurance. From the little he had seen of Simon while unloading the crated grapes in the marketplace, it was clear that he possessed these desirable traits. He admired the youth's slender but broad-shouldered physique, and thought that it would be put to good use. The harvesting season would last three more very strenuous weeks. The work consisted of picking the grapes from the terraced vineyard, collecting the fruit in bins, crating it and shipping it to the marketplace.

Panos was very proud of his sweet, dark grapes, and they fetched a good price from the stall keepers. However, time was of the essence, as overripe fruit went off quickly and grapes that were picked but not promptly marketed developed fruit-skin wrinkles and did not sell well. He had a skill for growing his grapes, inherited through many generations of vineyard ownership. But he was aware that he was not getting any younger, and help was needed during the merciless harvest season. If this lad lasts for three weeks of hard work, thought Panos, I will consider it a stroke of good fortune.

Recalling his job interview with a grin, Simon thought of the money he had saved by not buying a suit and tie, inasmuch as such job-interview attire was seldom seen around these parts. Moreover, he definitely could not complain about his wages. Simon's handsome pay packet arrived promptly each Friday, with drachma notes carefully folded into a small brown envelope, his name proudly printed on it in Greek characters. Working for Panos was hard, but certainly not underpaid.

In the back of his mind, Simon knew that complaining about the hardship of this labour was little more than a well-rehearsed habit. He had acquired this dubious practice from his workmates in London, at the geriatric mental hospital. When presented with a strenuous task at work, they were in the habit of complaining bitterly and then dragging their feet through the job at hand. In fact, he admitted to himself, wiping the muddy, brownish sweat from his forehead, his return to grey and rainy London and work at the hospital could wait.

The young Englishman's arrival was welcomed by Panos's friends and family. Simon had a quiet, undemanding and somewhat bashful manner about him, which they liked. In addition, he was respected for his strength and hard work. At first, Panos laid down a mattress for him in the guest room. This arrangement seemed satisfactory for a few days. But one evening, when Panos returned from the vineyard, Ephdoxia, his wife, told him that she was a little concerned about their young daughter, Sophia. At seventeen, the young lady was attractive, naïve and rapidly becoming infatuated with the young "Ingliss."

Ephdoxia wanted the guest to leave the house: people would soon start talking and it was inappropriate to let a mature Englishman and young Sophia sleep under the same roof. In Ephdoxia's mind, things could easily get out of hand. The mixed combination of female teenage hormones and Mediterranean passion, mingled with the English vacation spirit, was a recipe for disaster. Panos and Ephdoxia debated the issue hotly. Reaching no agreement with his wife over the matter, Panos was upset at having to deal with such aggravating matters in the midst of harvest. He strolled to the village taverna in search of a sympathetic ear.

The taverna was owned by Manos, Panos's cousin and a recognised troubleshooter. Having listened to his cousin's burdensome load, Manos poured them both a measure of ouzo, watered down to a cloudy white. As they sipped their drinks, he said, "Strong and healthy young men are becoming scarce in this part of the world."

Panos nodded in agreement. His own son, Nikos, had left home some years ago. Panos had failed to persuade him to stay and work in the vineyard. Nikos lived at the port town, and when not at sea, frequently visited the village on holiday. He loved sailing and had joined the merchant fleet as a naval officer. Panos was proud of him, but Nikos's departure had intensified Panos's desire to find a successor.

"Soon this village will become an old-age sanatorium," replied Panos. He had been painfully aware of the tendency of younger people to leave the villages, favouring secure employment in town or abroad. The younger generation had moved away from tilling the land, or fishing. They had perceived success as doing well away from rural, agricultural Greece.

"Make the Englishman stay!" Manos urged. "Hang on to him if you can. He is very good and strong."

"How do I do that?" asked Panos.

Manos laughed and refilled their ouzo glasses with another measure of misty white. "How does one attract the bee? Try with honey and blossom sweetness, of course!"

He winked and said, "Here is a plan for you: Convince the Englishman that he is important and special. Pay him well and make him feel that he is your partner. That way, he will stay here and help you farm your grapes for a long time."

"I cannot let him stay in my house any more. The way Sophia looks at him, it won't be long before he finds his way to her bed at night."

Manos sipped his ouzo slowly, raking his curly hair back with his fingers. He smiled knowingly at his cousin and said, "I have an idea of how we can solve all these problems." And conspiracy was underway.

Panos held the rusty old Schmeisser submachine gun by its leather strap. It dangled awkwardly in midair in front of Simon's eyes. Simon looked at the weapon in curious disbelief. It looks like an exhibit from a war museum, he thought to himself. He had never in his life handled any type of firearm, let alone a small machine gun. This particular specimen was encrusted with oil that had dried up a long time ago and seemed solid with rust. Fortunately, he thought, there didn't appear to be any ammunition attached to it.

"Smeissers," said Panos in German-Greek. He beckoned Simon to come and take the gun. He had carefully stored it since the German troops left it behind during their hasty retreat almost forty years ago. Panos had always felt that it would be put to good use one day. In the intervening years, Panos had gained a certain sense of security knowing that the weapon was hidden in his attic. Perhaps he had felt that it was a measure of safety against an unexpected return of the Nazis.

Manos had suggested that the young Englishman be assigned watchman duties and issued with a firearm. The purpose of this appointment was to bolster the young man's self-esteem and sense of importance. At first, Panos had objected to the idea that Simon should be put in possession of the machine gun.

"How can I give a casual foreign worker an automatic weapon which we have been hiding from the Nazis for forty years?"

Now it was his cousin's turn to be puzzled. "First, you don't trust this English boy in the same house as your daughter. Then, you claim that he is such a great asset in the vineyard that you may consider him as a future successor. Now, you still don't want to honour him by giving him the gun that you never use anyway. You know what, your wife is right. You are a fool!"

And so it came about that Simon was in possession of the rusty Schmeisser and entrusted with the novel watchman's duty.

He woke up in the stone hut, which was now his new home. The lodging came together with the new job as watchman and the old automatic gun, in addition to his vineyard task. He was tired and his eyelids felt leaden. His palate was dry, but there was no water in the hut to quench his thirst. He had run out of drinking water the night before and would have to wait for Panos to bring a fresh supply, which he carried in two jerry cans on the back of a donkey. As he had been too tired to walk to the village, he had made do with the coarse wine that the workers kept in a jug in the hut. The semi-fermented plonk had produced an inevitable headache and a sensation of thirst. Moreover, he had a distinct discomfort in his stomach, and he did not know whether it was from drinking the wine or the unpalatable food. Today was going to be even more of a physical ordeal since he had started the day with a hangover.

Simon had little love for the Greek dishes and no taste for the muddy coffee, which they always drank in tiny white china cups. The food gave him indigestion, and he frequently suffered from an upset stomach. At first, he thought that perhaps his digestion problems had something to do with differences between English and Greek intestinal flora. However, he had to dismiss this theory, since he had suffered from no stomach problems prior to arriving at the village. Finally, he admitted to himself that the food was simply awful. This realisation made him feel guilty, since he knew that in most cases Sophia was responsible for preparing it. He did not wish to offend her, as he was well aware of her attempts to please him. So he ate what she cooked and suffered the consequences.

Simon mused about Sophia as he walked towards the taverna that evening. He realised that Panos and Ephdoxia were concerned about his budding relationship with their daughter. He had found Sophia very attractive, and was aware of a sexual tension between the two of them. He looked forward to the brief encounters with her while he ate his midday meal; intimacy was definitely building up between them. She cooked his food, served his dinner and laundered the clothes that he brought back from the day's labour at the vineyard. But they never engaged in conversation. This was probably due more to bashfulness than to the language barrier.

In the evenings, he felt her watching him climb up the terraced mountain path leading to the vineyard and his hut. He imagined kissing her and then taking off her white blouse, letting her wonderful breasts spring free of the garment, which at all times threatened to burst under the pressure.

Simon considered it both childish and amusing that Panos and his wife had banished him from their house. It was naïve of them to think that removing him from the house at night was going to prevent the relationship from developing any further. In fact, they had actually made it easier for him. All he needed to do now was persuade Sophia to come to the stone hut.

A small group of villagers were sitting on low wicker chairs in the square facing the taverna as Simon approached. Some were sipping coffee from tiny cups. Others were chatting or playing backgammon. The sliding sound of the disc-shaped play pieces against the board's elevated wooden edge and the rolling dice produced a gentle clicking noise. Several well-worn play boards were active, each with a circle of spectators and advisors. When Simon arrived, there appeared to be a short pause in the taverna's routine. Then, someone clapped him on the shoulder. A voice in the taverna's background shouted, "*Yasu* Simon!" Manos poured out a small glass of Greek brandy for him, and all faces were smiling.

Simon sat down to sip his drink and asked for a large bottle of mineral water. A young fellow who sometimes worked in the vineyard with him made a shaping gesture with his hands, which resembled the contour of a coke bottle. He called out "Sophia," and laughed. Simon blushed, but joined in the laughter. There was no sign of Sophia. Surveying the all-male crowd of the taverna, he realised that she probably would not come to such a place. He picked up the water bottle, paid for it and waved good-bye to the friendly faces around him. As he approached the path leading towards the terraced hillside, he noticed Sophia standing by the road, her shoulders wrapped in a woolen shawl to protect her from the autumn evening's chill. He quickened his step and approached her.

"*Kalinichta*, Simon."

"*Kalinichta*, Sophia. How are you?"

She obviously did not want to follow him up the path, but held his hand briefly and then scurried off in the direction of her home.

Simon's pulse quickened; he wished she would stay. Maybe next time, he thought to himself. He walked quickly up the dirt road, found the door to his hut in the darkness and lit the kerosene lamp that Panos had given him. The yellow and orange flames gave off a romantic glow, which made him feel lonely. He wished Sophia were with him. He lay on his back and looked at the old Schmeisser hanging by its strap from a hook on the back of the wooden door. The flickering light of the lamp gave it an evil look, and he took it off the door, handling it with distrust, as he was still scared that it might spurt bullets. In spite of its apparent obsolescence, he was unquiet about the weapon. He hid it under the mattress.

Panos arrived at the taverna a while after the Englishman had left. The jovial group around the backgammon boards had told him that his protégé had left a short while ago. He made his way to the counter and asked Manos, "Have you seen Sophia this evening?"

"Sophia will soon leave home if you cannot find a good match for her," answered Manos and poured his cousin some ouzo. "I told her to go up the path and wait for the Ingliss, when he goes up to the hut with his water bottle."

Panos emptied his glass and looked at his cousin quizzically. "What has the Ingliss and his water got to do with Sophia's future plans in the village?"

Manos laughed and refilled his glass. "Are you happy with the way we handled the situation with Ephdoxia, sent the Ingliss to the hut and got everything under control here without blemishing your daughter's reputation?" Panos nodded and sipped his drink. "Now," continued Manos, "Convince him to marry Sophia and then he will stay here for good!"

"You're crazy – he doesn't speak a word of Greek!" exclaimed Panos.

He noticed that a group had quietly formed around them,

listening in on their conversation. Manos looked at everyone and then told Panos: "Since when does a man need to speak Greek just to get married? You're crazy yourself if you let him go. You see, this way you can keep both him and your daughter!" Panos looked around him and saw all faces nodding in agreement. Obviously, Manos had extended the conspiracy to heights and depths that even Panos had not dared think of before. As farfetched and as mad as this plan seemed, he had to agree that his cousin had been ahead of the game, and right so far. Thus, he had little choice but to spend the rest of the evening drinking and listening to Manos.

Simon could not quite put his finger on how or when it became publicly evident to all that he would marry Sophia and stay in the village. Certainly, as the language barrier prevented it, no one had ever told him in so many words that this was the master plan. However, the combination of hints, the general atmosphere and the behaviour of those involved strongly indicated what was on everyone's mind. He felt that the social pressure was gradually building up around him. The grape harvest was in its final quarter, as was obvious from the remaining vines still to be worked.

In spite of the almost complete lack of verbal communication, everyone was treating him like family, making the insinuation quite clear. They wanted him to marry Sophia and stay. She looked after his clothes and his food and waited for him outside the taverna in the evening. They would then walk together to where the mountain path met the perimeter of the village outskirts. He would make an attempt to coax her into going to the hut with him by waltzing around her and pulling her towards the path, but eventually she always laughed off his courtship dance and walked home, leaving him to trail alone up the terraces to the hut.

The thought of Sophia warmed his heart. He loved her beautiful dark skin and perfect teeth, found her altogether sexy and longed to get her to spend time alone with him. However, although she spoke a few words of English and he could, by that time, utter some simple Greek sentences, they hadn't really spoken to each other. The continuing lack of intimacy disturbed him.

She was attractive and he longed for her, but he remarked to himself with amusement that her mother had a hint of a dark moustache and was rather broad about the backside. A little off-putting, he thought. But how many of his previous girlfriends' mothers had fitted this same pattern? It seemed to be immaterial whether they came from the Mediterranean basin, the English Channel or anywhere else in the world.

However, once the idea of marrying this girl and living in rural Greece dawned on him, Simon's mind began to work overtime. At first, the idea seemed ridiculous and far-fetched. How could a thinking, intelligent person who was brought up in civilised Britain possibly consider choosing such a primitive way of life? He had little in common with these people and their land. They were thinking of him as a future son-in-law but did not even care about his basic welfare. There was no running water. Washing and toilet facilities were a problem, and so was the lack of electricity. Drinking water had to be carried from the village. He could not fathom the mentality of people who seemed to want him as part of their family, yet let him grapple with such appalling living conditions. Perhaps they were testing his endurance? Their lives were not austere to that extent, so why put him through such a test? Simon was baffled.

On the other hand, his rented living quarters in London could not exactly be described as luxurious. The flat was damp and shabby, with continual plumbing problems, a greedy, sour-faced landlord, poor insulation and annoying electrical meters that devoured ten-pence coins at an unbelievable rate. He found the constant drizzle and grey skies depressing. The warm, stale air that accompanied the endless daily tube rides to and from work choked him. How could that be healthy?

And when he thought it through, he realized he was fed up with psychiatric nursing. In fact, this extended holiday in Greece had come after a particularly difficult stretch of time in one of the wards. Some of the geriatric inmates had become abusive and violent. In particular, he recalled an incident when one of them had hurled a bedpan half full of urine, soaking him and other staff with foul-smelling, straw-coloured liquid. Reflecting back on why he had opted for psychiatric nursing, he remembered that one of the deciding factors had been the shorter and relatively easier course of training, as compared to medical training. Now, he regretted his choice. He wondered if poor planning of his career options was the reason for wishing to give up life in England in favour of becoming a Greek villager.

Simon tried playing devil's advocate and carefully considered if he would really miss anything about life in London. Rugby weekends at Twickenham would be irreplaceable, he knew. He still played for a local neighbourhood team and took part in ten-pint pub crawls after a Saturday game. He recalled, however, that he had grown to dislike the inevitable beer on Friday and Saturday nights, and lunchtime on Sunday. Most of his crowd drank far too much and suffered for it. There was an uneasy feeling that lingered in his mind about the quality of London leisure and weekend entertainment. It did seem somewhat empty when regarded from far away. He was not quite certain that he truly missed it. The more he thought about his life back in London, the more confused he felt.

Sophia too felt uncertain and anxious about the situation. "How can you be sure that he will ever want to marry me?" she asked her mother.

Ephdoxia thought for a while, trying to come up with a clever, reassuring reply.

"Ask your father" was the best she could manage. Ridden with anxiety, Sophia went looking for her father. She found both him and Manos sitting and sipping coffee at the taverna.

Approaching them quietly, she asked softly, "Father, is the English fellow really going to marry me?"

Manos smiled at her and asked, "Does he look at you every day?"

"He cannot take his eyes off my body and he keeps trying to drag me to the hut in the vineyard every evening."

"You mustn't walk more than halfway to the hut with him. Things will be all right." He winked, and Sophia, feeling no less anxious, tried to tell herself that although her mother always said that both her father and Manos were just a pair of blundering fools, she should trust their wisdom and experience.

Sophia clearly wanted this wedding to take place. She liked Simon and thought that he would be a warm and considerate husband. And a huge village feast with lots of guests from abroad sounded like a wonderful idea. They would travel and visit England. She had heard about London, and the idea of visiting Buckingham Palace and Harrods excited her imagination. She tried hard to calm herself down and went to collect her future spouse's dry laundry off the line.

That night, Simon had a particularly nasty stomachache and a bout of diarrhoea. He had run out of the hut but had been caught short and had soiled his underwear. Cursing the food, he realised that there was not enough water to rinse his dirty underwear with, nor could he leave it for Sophia to wash. He buried the soiled pants at the far end of the vineyard, covering the sepulchre with earth and packing the dirt tight with his feet.

To his dismay, one of the village mongrels dug up the buried undergarment early the following morning. The hound also had the presence of mind to cheerfully return the offering to its master, leaving it in full daylight on the hut's threshold. A few villagers who had come to work in the vineyard that morning were trying to stifle their giggles at the sight of the beshitted underwear on his doorstep.

Simon could not hide his embarrassment. He glimpsed at the ridiculous Schmeisser, its muzzle protruding from under his mattress, before leaving the hut to join the other workers. An unpleasant weight lay heavy between the midst of his chest and the pit of his bowel during the whole day, obscuring his mood. What a fine figure of a bridegroom I must make, he thought, feeling the humiliation closing in and choking him. He found this feeling intolerable. In his mind's eye, all were watching the back of his trousers at all times.

On Friday morning, his misgivings about the cultural differences, the language barrier and his continued disgust with the quality of food that he ate had gotten the better of him. His mind was going around in circles. He could not recognise his laidback, affable self in this state of troubled mind and irritated bowel. The thought of Sophia and a delusional Greek wedding in a strange land suddenly seemed remote and frightening. Combined with his injured dignity after the soiled-underwear episode, Simon had reached a solid conclusion that he really could not go on. Trying hard to regain rationality, he sat down in the hut and thought to himself: It's time to take stock.

There was sufficient money in his pocket to comfortably travel to Athens and get a flight ticket back to London, or anywhere he wished to go. He had made no verbal promise to anyone, regarding any commitment whatsoever. The harvest that he felt morally obliged to finish was all but over. A voice inside his head was screaming for him to get out.

Having put his thoughts in order, Simon proceeded to collect all his belongings and packed them into the rucksack. Cautiously, he removed the Schmeisser from underneath the bedding and placed it over the mattress, now bare of his sleeping bag. Convincing himself that he was doing the right thing, he waited for his employer to arrive.

Panos arrived with his weekly pay packet, folded in the usual envelope. He saw Simon's backpack and slowly realised that his master plan had failed to produce the desired result, despite Manos's brilliant scheme. The disappointment was clearly visible in his face, but he said nothing. The two walked silently and gloomily together to the village. Upon reaching the vicinity of the house, Simon requested that Panos drive him to the bus stop on the main road, but the Greek refused. Without argument, the youth waved a perfunctory good-bye and made his way on foot.

It was early October and the air was crisp and pleasant. The walk was long, but Simon did not mind at all. He felt no anger towards Panos for turning down his request for a lift in the Peugeot truck. He was sad to be leaving Sophia, and plagued with remorse over how he must be hurting her. But with every step he took, Simon felt a heavy weight gradually lifting off his chest, melting away into the autumn breeze and giving him a new sense of freedom.

Beirut, 1982: Theatre of the Absurd
1982

A suntanned arm appeared out of nowhere inside the public telephone booth. A hand gently disconnected the call before the dialing was completed. The slim, dark-skinned fellow in a beige civilian safari suit had an earphone which was connected to a tiny radio set by an elastic spiral cable that ran from his ear and through his lapel. He apologised to the surprised reserve soldier who had started the phone call to his wife, and explained, "I'm really sorry. Absolutely no outgoing calls are allowed from the port at this time. These are strict and severe orders. Don't even think of telephoning, and remind all your friends too."

Before the uniformed soldier could ask any questions, the man in the safari suit had vanished into the night.

That night the ship's hold was loaded with our regiment's armoured vehicles. Troop carriers and smaller vehicles were covered with camouflage netting on the upper decks. All this preparation had ended before dawn, and by early morning we had already sailed out of the Ashdod port heading north. The early-August Mediterranean gently rocked the boat as the coast of Israel slowly disappeared into the morning haze. Cardboard ration boxes were opened, their dry content supplemented from the ship's kitchen with fresh cheese and vegetables. The troops ate, or dozed off on the decks under the nets, making up for lost sleep during the long, busy night.

Speculations, rumours and theories buzzed in the air. We weren't just a group of regular army soldiers in wait of operational activity, but thirty-year-old reservists, most of whom had served together in the same regiment for seven or eight years. Many had young families, some had budding careers, and a large proportion of the chain of command was still at various stages of higher education or professional training.

Rumours spoke of shelling at our destination port in west Beirut, or of close combat with PLO men. A wealth of well-founded and less well-founded tales prevailed, as they typically do.

During the briefing, we were told that the plan was to reach Beirut at 1:00 a.m. Once the ship's landing ramp touched the jetty, all vehicles had to clear the decks within minutes. This was in order to avoid a prolonged vulnerable stay in the port area, close to the PLO stronghold. Tanks would go first, and the lighter vehicles would follow. I was to be in charge of getting everyone off the ship in the prearranged order and making certain that all vehicles were promptly rolling on tracks or wheels out of the port, due northeast towards the hills near Junia. Yossi Fromm, the regiment's CO, was detailed to head the column. As I was in charge of the rescue part of the mission, my task was to bring up the rear. Thus, I was provided with a Dodge all-terrain command car. Traveling along with me was a team of reserve army mechanics supplemented with an infantry security guard corps.

The ship's captain pointed out that it was essential that he sail out of Beirut's port no later than half an hour after the landing ramp was opened. He had to leave Lebanese territorial waters before daybreak. This left but a narrow margin for error and demanded a swift, efficient exit from the ship's hold.

After another rations meal on the upper decks, we prepared for landing. On the vehicle ramp in the ship's bowel, the tanks were tightly lined up track beside track, guns kissing the back of the tank at their front – a long row of exhaust pipes joined by armoured plate undercarriages. My team hopped from vehicle to vehicle, checking that all operating systems were in working order and ready to go.

As we approached Beirut, everyone got into position. The air in the ship's haul was hot and stale with a heavy, malodorous mixture of gun oil and engine fumes. The bright white neon lighting below deck was replaced by wartime red landing lights. We wore helmets and shrapnel jackets as well as our full gun belts and waited for the ship's landing. Our faces seemed bright with sweat, which reflected a red shine in the emergency light – a surreal dimension that belonged in Hollywood war films, not in our normal lives.

Anxiety and uncertainty loomed over our crucial questions: What awaits us at the west-Beirut port upon arrival? Will there be active contact with hostile forces when we land? Is the port area under PLO shelling? Is the northbound route to Junia free of overt and hidden enemy lurking for prey?

An ominous, pregnant silence prevailed during the moments just before the huge solid metal gate in our front turned the ship's lower hold into a landing ramp. Fromm, our CO, stood by his jeep, his face shining under the reddish light. Deep lines grooved between his nose and the corners of his mouth. Gun grease and dirt stained his brow; he looked serious. I had known Fromm well for the better part of eleven years, both as soldier and as a reserve-force commander. The burden that lay on his shoulders was enormous. Every man's life on board was like his own. I stood a few feet from him, and his eyes caught my gaze. I winked at him in an attempt to lighten the somber atmosphere. Fromm allowed himself a brief fragment of a smile and a nod of acknowledgement.

The screeching of heavy chains and a metallic thud signaled the landing ramp's lowering and touching ground. The ship's hold now became continuous with the port's concrete pier. Beirut's sky was clear with a silver two-thirds moon hanging high above, and all was quiet around us. All at once the tank engines roared to life, momentarily creating an impregnable smoke screen over our mobile column. My command vehicle moved into position at the head of the column. Once clear of the landing ramp I stranded it on the quay to supervise swift evacuation from the ship's hold towards the port's gate.

The landing area was completely quiet. Only the grating of the tank tracks on the concrete and the powerful diesel engines' rumble broke the night's silence. Fromm stood next to me, and beside him the artillery brigadier held himself aloof by his jeep. He sported a beard, wore full regular army colonel insignia on his shoulders and stood stone-faced, with one leg on the running board of the jeep. Obviously, he wanted Fromm's regiment out of the port and in position, where it would be under his army's control.

We sweated under the heavy gear in the hot, humid night. Standing next to us on the same quay was a youngish fellow with curly hair. He wore an army shirt with no insignia over a pair of shorts, and stood in open sandals with an AK-47 assault rifle slung almost nonchalantly over his shoulder. On his belt was a compact wireless radio set with a mouthpiece at the end of a coiled rubber cable. In all likelihood, he belonged to a GSS (general security service) unit or another special outfit; he looked calm and relaxed. As if detached from the pandemonium around him, he exchanged a few words with Fromm. I wondered who he was, a soldier or a civilian agent. Why was he free of a helmet, protective gear and boots while we all sweated away? What was his specific role in the mission at hand? He probably belongs in another movie, and is just making a brief guest appearance in ours, I told myself.

My thoughts were interrupted by Fromm. "Engine failure in one of the tanks on the boat," he shouted. The bearded brigadier, too, was noticeably uptight. The ship's captain was adamant about clearing out of the port on schedule. He was prepared to throw the truculent machine off his boat and, if need be, into the sea, with a Caterpillar D-9 bulldozer.

"Give me a minute," I said and ran off into the ship's hold. The stubborn tank stood by the hold's side and obstructed the passage of yet another tank behind it. The engine would not start. I unhinged a heavy-duty 24-volt electrical cable and connected both tanks' batteries. A tank mechanics' sergeant major stood nearby. I asked him to get into the tank's driver hatch and try to start the engine under the second tank's power, while I revved up the other tank's diesel engine. He eyed me with reluctance and said, "I'm a workshop chief. Driving tanks isn't my job. I'm not getting into the driver's hatch."

I couldn't believe my ears and threatened to break both his arms unless he got into the hatch and started the engine in three seconds. He got the message, and the dead engine roared into life in no time. Quickly disconnecting the 24-volt cable, I signaled the two drivers forward and got both tanks out. Much to the captain's relief, the ship's hold now stood empty of all our regiment's vehicles.

Fromm, the brigadier and the captain stood outside by the ramp. The brigadier appeared much less anxious; he shook my hand warmly. Fromm had regained his old spirits and complained that my minute took ninety seconds. "You're losing it, my boy.

You must be getting old," he said. I confirmed his suspicion, reminded him that we were born the same year, and got into my command car. The delay caused both tanks to be left behind the mobile armoured column, already moving out of the port's gate on the Beirut–Junia carriageway.

Fromm teamed up with the tank that worked well and followed the convoy's trail, rapidly overtaking the column. I ordered the mechanics team to quickly go over the tank's engine systems; once they were finished the tank crew drove away immediately while the rescue team and I followed in the command car. Consulting my map, we followed the signposts northbound to Junia.

It was 1:30 a.m., thirty minutes after the ramp had touched the pier. We had left the port's perimeter and were on schedule. Traffic seemed busy in spite of the late hour. The road was wide, with three lanes in each direction. Drivers around us gave the tank no more than a perfunctory look. The majority of vehicles were civilian, but some strange hybrids drove along with us. These were normal vehicles or small trucks with cut roofs and back seats that were converted into makeshift machine-gun posts. Such vehicles were manned by armed men in camouflage fatigues, or military bottoms and black T-shirts. It was hard to tell who they were, friend or foe. Obviously, at that time a host of small militias freely operated in Beirut and were loyal mostly to themselves.

We travelled at a slow pace, keeping close to the tank, which stalled from time to time. The vehicles with open tops and armed militia men largely ignored us, overtaking the slower moving tank and accompanying command car. When nearing a spaghetti junction on the northern outskirts of the city, the tank's engine died out again and we came to a halt. At that point, it was clear that we had a recurrent malfunction problem with the engine. I stepped on board the tank with the mechanic, who opened the engine plates and began rummaging about the fuel system hoses.

Leaving him to it, I made certain that two of my guards were positioned on either side of the ascending lanes in the junction, leaving as few margins for surprises as I could. I radioed Fromm and reported the failure and delay, and our exact position in code. "Bastard tank. Give me a progress report in ten. Over and out." By his reply I understood that he was otherwise engaged, but also concerned about our situation which he could do little about.

The mechanic reported that the Cummins diesel had an air bubble in the fuel system. One of the rubber hoses was faulty and he had replaced it with a new one. Yet the diesel needed to purge off the air pocket, since that model was not equipped with an automatic electrical fuel pump. The technique for performing that task was quite simple and consisted of draining half a litre of diesel oil from the fuel tank and refilling it through the open hose. The fuel tank was equipped with a small nipple tap for this purpose. Unfortunately, it had been damaged and somehow smashed into deformity. It could not be turned open and the diesel fluid could not be otherwise reached. Our command-car motor was gasoline operated and draining it would be of no use. We were stuck.

A quick evaluation of our situation was not too optimistic. We were alone in the middle of a busy traffic artery with unknown hostile forces within reach. Staying in that position for too long increased the risk odds. We were well advised to get away as soon as possible. I looked around and spotted a small petrol station under the concrete flyover at the lower level of the junction. Asking one of the guards to accompany me, I got hold of a three-litre plastic can and walked over to the station. There were no cars fueling up, and two fellows in short sleeves sat on small wicker chairs near a lit glass cubicle playing with amber-beaded string chains. The neon lamps under the concrete bridge gave off a bluish light, giving our helmeted sweaty faces an unhealthy pallor. I approached the fellows and asked, "*Fee diesel* (Do you have any diesel)?" One of them pointed to a pump that had a large sign over it: Diesel Oil. I took out the nozzle and filled the plastic can. Getting back to the men, I extracted my wallet from under the shrapnel vest and took out a five-shekel note. The attendant examined the foreign currency, and then looked at our faces under the full battle gear at two o'clock in the morning. "*Ma'alesh* (Never mind)," he said, and handed back the bill.

We hurried back to the tank. Using the diesel oil that we had obtained, we purged the offending air bubble from the fuel system, completely fixing the engine failure. We were rolling again, this time without stalling delays. After a few kilometers, we found Fromm waiting for us by his jeep at the junction where we turned east. We stopped briefly. Fromm's soiled face appeared even more worried than it had been on the boat. I briefly reported the petrol-station incident, which made his face crinkle into a smile. "I was worried about you," he said, and slapped my shoulder. Now that we had all collected under his control he seemed more relaxed.

It was three o'clock in the morning when we began climbing uphill, driving through a dormant Christian village. The ascent was cobblestoned and winding, the tank's metal tracks on the hard surface turning the ride into a delicate skid-and-grate operation. While taking a corner, we noticed that one of the walls of the house had been partly demolished. A tank from our regiment had skidded and accidentally hit the wall with its side, breaking a hole in the stone latticework. The furniture and TV inside the home were visible through the hole, but the living room didn't appear to have been damaged. Fromm said that the higher command had apologised and promised to repair the damage. In fact, on my next trip down that road, I noticed that the wall had been rebuilt. The army engineering corps had recruited a crew from the Galilee that specialised in stone masonry in order to comply with the promise made to the villagers.

The dry facts could not prevent the tale of the broken wall from becoming a myth. Days later the rumoured version of the incident told about the tank's gun penetrating into the bedroom, interrupting the activity there. The legends revolved around the tank's deep incursion into the villagers' privacy. There obviously was no restriction or nonsense tax on the wartime imagination of soldiers.

At the top of the hill, our regiment was deployed near the Christian militia's base. We were stopped at the barrier by a Christian Phalanges soldier who wore a large gold cross on a chain around his neck, and underneath it another gold chain with the name "Pierre" on it. Pierre spoke French and showed great interest in the double-magazine clip attached to my short-version M-16 rifle. He made no excuse about asking me to give it to him. I politely refused, using the kindest French that I could muster up for the occasion. I could not part with that particular operational item then. He didn't seem offended, but took a rolled wad of US dollars out of his pocket and offered me fifty dollars for the clip. I shook my head and said no. Pierre took out a hundred dollars and offered it without even thinking twice. At that stage, I told him that no way could he buy our military gear. Yet I would get him a clip like mine later, free of charge. That seemed to satisfy him for the time and he let us in, lifting the weighted barrier.

I could now better understand the vast negotiating potential that we had with the Christian Phalanges militias.

It was nearly 4:00 a.m. when we got to the area in which the regiment had set camp that night. Dead tired, we got into our sleeping bags and fell asleep.

Buzzing flies and general activity woke us up at about seven o'clock. One of our men couldn't get a troop carrier's engine to start and was urgently looking for the chief mechanic, who was lying beside me. He crawled out of his sleeping bag wearing a

T-shirt, walked over and opened the engine hood. Spotting the problem, he called for help as he needed an extra pair of hands to tighten a loose belt. I got up and went over to help him.

We had the engine purring in no time and while shutting the engine hood we heard an angry shout behind us. Last night's brigadier had driven by in his jeep and apparently balked at seeing us in our T-shirts. He stuck his bearded face out of the car window and screamed, "Are you two ready to stand for court-martial now?"

I realised that he was even more sleep deprived than we were, but still couldn't understand why or how he found the time to add discipline sergeant major to his already heavy responsibilities as brigadier. Nonetheless, I approached his window and said: "Excuse me sir, perhaps we can borrow the ship captain's bulldozer and throw this troop carrier into the harbour's water as well? It's not far off." Memory of the previous night's tank engine failure probably dawned on him then, and he drove off angrily saying nothing, his rear wheels kicking up earth behind him. His day had obviously not started well.

Fromm gathered us and gave a short talk about the nature of the war we were fighting against the PLO, who had taken South Lebanon hostage and threatened northern Israel intolerably. He spoke of the Christian Phalanges allies in the camp and in the village next door. Finally, he highlighted the obvious: one knows how a war begins, but not how it ends.

The days following our landing entailed occasional firing at targets belonging to PLO strongholds in west Beirut, or their collaborators. We also liaised with Christian officers and raided several houses that, according to what they suspected or knew, sheltered terrorists or hostile war materials. The front was still active, with PLO forces cornered but well deployed and supported in west Beirut. Bitter debate had split the public at home, whether to attack the terrorist organisation at the cost of their Lebanese human shield, or negotiate some sort of an evacuation deal. The politicians were hotly arguing with each other.

While the regiment was busy handling our part of the fighting, we worked closely with Christian officers from the nearby base. In spite of the close collaboration, we couldn't fathom the nature of their soldiering habits. For instance, a massive exodus of BMW and Alfa Romeo cars from the Christian camp's parking lot was a daily spectacle around three o'clock in the afternoon, leaving a very thin garrison behind.

We wondered where these soldiers were going. The answer was "the American University of Beirut." All the same, they were great partners for going out to town, drinking and dining. Yet the question remained: How reliable would they be as our backup under fire?

Public controversy regarding the Lebanon campaign leaked into the regiment as our prolonged stay became static, creating an unhealthy atmosphere. Given the hazy goal of the war they were fighting, reserve soldiers in their thirties became demoralised. Distress, impatience and lack of focus created an uncomfortable feeling of confusion as time went by.

Although this war differed considerably from the previous one in which many of us fought for our survival in 1973, it was war nonetheless. Complacency and carelessness could cost dearly.

Reserve psychologists were recruited by the military command to deal with this problem at field level. They talked to the forces daily, and organised sightseeing activities, giving a focal objective to those who showed the need for it. However, the whole environment was dangerously loose. Beirut was a smuggler's paradise. Dealers and salesmen peddled VCR sets, electronic goods and whiskey at a third of their cost in Israel. Commerce thrived in spite of severe military police warnings.

Images of untidy Israeli reservists cutting deals with Lebanese counterfeit bandits reflected poorly on us as a fighting force. An unwholesome and degenerating state was developing, with contraband goods piling up beside soldiers' weapons and combat gear.

I recalled a discipline problem arising during a reserve stretch a few years prior to the 1982 war, with several regiment soldiers driven to play poker for significant stakes while on active reserve service. Fromm, who censured gambling in uniform, had dealt harshly with it. Yet Lebanon seemed to exceed his capabilities of tight control and personal responsibility. Obviously, the implications of our stay in Beirut on the attitude of the reservists had to be dealt with at a higher military level. Apparently, top military command registered this phenomenon only post-factum. The failure to deal with soldiers let loose inside a nonhostile foreign milieu was later addressed. Yet we saw the potentially problematic effect soon after the incursion. Fortunately, our regiment paid no price in blood for this folly.

Four weeks into Beirut, and I was allowed a few days' leave in order to complete an overdue biochemistry exam. I couldn't make the military bus transport back to Beirut, so I drove to the Rosh Hanikra border crossing, walking over to the Lebanese side.

Going back to Beirut after spending three days at home and on the university campus felt out of place and awkward. While walking across the border and back into the Lebanon war reality, I almost wished that I hadn't been granted leave.

Military orders allowed travel in pairs, either on army transport or in civilian cars. I caught a ride with an army truck to the outskirts of Tyre, alighting at a junction together with a young parachute-force sergeant. I suddenly realised that we were alone with no Israeli military presence around us. This state of affairs felt unduly dangerous and potentially ambush prone. We couldn't defend ourselves against such an event. I shared this thought with the paratrooper, telling him that we should take the first opportunity to move away. A Lebanese Peugeot car stopped for us. It had a blue Madonna sticker on the windshield and the driver wore a golden cross. He looked about forty years old, was pleasant and helpful and said that he was going to Beirut. Speaking French, he showed an interest in us and asked about our families back home.

We reached the beautiful, though battle-scarred, business centre in downtown Beirut. The paratrooper spotted and signaled a vehicle from his outfit, and we asked the Lebanese driver to stop for us. I made use of the paratrooper's vehicle's radio set, dialing in our regiment's frequency. Fifteen minutes later, Redhead Abe from my regiment picked me up from the post in his jeep. In retrospect, the trip from the border to Beirut had been unnecessary and probably dangerous.

These were Bachir Gemayel's election days, and when the Lebanese parliament voted him in as head of state, huge festivities broke out. The starting point was the Phalanges base and the village. Christian soldiers on the roof of the base's main building opened the festivities by shooting into the air. Our first reaction was to lie low and put our shrapnel jackets and helmets on, but we soon understood that the firing was an outpour of joy. Young girls from the village came by attired in wedding garb and gave out sugared almonds and tiny cupfuls of Zahlawi arak. In the regiment deployed next to us, however, the doctor treated two reserve soldiers lightly wounded by falling trajectory bullets from the "fantasia" shooting frenzy.

As history books record, the end of that particular celebration was a bitter one – Bachir Gemayel was killed a few days later by a Moslem-operated car bomb. Gemayel's assassination threw Lebanon into dangerous instability. A bloodthirsty Phalanges reprisal followed in the refugee camps Sabra and Shatila, creating a far-reaching international scandal.

We had finished our tour of reserve duty when Arafat's PLO gang was evacuated from Beirut to Tunis by sea. This time, only tanks and vehicles made their way back by boat. The men drove through the border and reached the Ashdod port by land. We arrived at night and it was dark when I off-loaded the last tank from the boat. I led the convoy to the hangar sheds in the military port, about two kilometers from the landing quay. Fromm, who was waiting for the last of his armoured column to arrive, was surprised to see me heading the parade. "How did you find me?" He asked. "Easy," I replied. "I followed your pretty tank tracks until I could smell you."

Jean-Louis Meets His Match
1989

Jean-Louis had an impressive nose. It occupied a normal, not a superlative, portion of his face; it was long and dominant. Its outstanding feature, however, was a slight protrusion at the end. The tip of the nose seemed to have a life of its own, almost like a bloodhound's muzzle. When actively curious, Jean-Louis' nostrils flared a little, like those of a hound of hunt. Not surprisingly, Jean-Louis' sense of smell was very keen, both in the olfactory sense and metaphorically. He had a great nose for art. If a work of art was genuine or had real quality and value, Jean-Louis' nostrils flared and told him so.

A native of a French town near the Swiss border, Jean-Louis was educated at the Sorbonne's art department. He resided and worked in Paris, breathing art and creating it in every possible way and in every genre. He produced, collected, practiced, searched, taught and lived for art in all forms.

Jean-Louis sketched and painted exquisitely, specialising in miniatures. Frequently he exhibited in museums and art galleries.

He also cooked passionately and creatively, occasionally dedicating himself to haute cuisine for unexpected lengths of time or to enterprising culinary ventures. Annette, his wife, was delighted by this, often being the recipient of her husband's delicious experiments.

Jean-Louis was also one of Paris's great judo masters. Holding the rank of fourth *dan*, he taught, practiced and enjoyed the martial art.

He spent his days working at the studio, shopping for foods, creating exotic recipes and never missing judo practice on the *tatami* mat, alone or with his colleagues. His life revolved around these three centres of interest, naturally moving from one to another to create what appeared to be a harmonious artistic trialogue.

Understanding Jean-Louis was no simple matter. Although there was nothing secretive or devious in the way in which he conducted his life, he was not predictable, least of all to himself. At certain times more intensively than at others.

One day, an art collector rang Jean-Louis and asked to see him. They met at a café of Jean-Louis' choice on Rue Vaugirard. The art collector expressed a wish to buy one of Jean-Louis' paintings, which he had seen at a private exhibition. The artist politely turned the collector down, telling him that the piece wasn't for sale at the time.

The collector seemed to be quite keen on acquiring the painting; he persisted and would not take no for an answer. Given an apologetic refusal, he gained the erroneous impression that Jean-Louis was perhaps trying to bump up the price. He said convincingly, "The gallery estimated the value of the work at twenty-five thousand francs. I'm prepared to give you fifty thousand."

Jean-Louis scratched his chin and replied, "Monsieur, the figure twenty-five thousand francs was estimated by the gallery's actuary only for insurance purposes. I sincerely appreciate your interest in my work and have no wish to offend you. If you need the piece for an exhibition, even a private one, I'll make arrangements with the gallery and lend it to you at no cost. But the gallery owners might have told you that I don't sell my art."

The collector answered, "In all truth, they did tell me exactly that. But I thought that perhaps you might need the money. Obviously, you don't."

"I make a living like anyone else. I am certainly aware of money and its role, even in the art field. But I don't sell my art."

"I'm curious now," said the collector. "If your art is so highly valued, but you never sell any of it, how then do you earn a living?"

Jean-Louis smiled. "I lecture at the university's art department and receive academic recognition as well as a pay cheque from them. But I won't lie to you. A large portion of my income comes from working as a consultant for art auction houses. Sotheby's, Christie's and various other private art dealers worldwide use my services. There is an art connoisseur's reputation I have to maintain and I always try to be fair and impartial. And yes, I receive a sizeable commission. Apart from auction houses, art collectors use my advice and services in assessing restoration costs. Usually my fee is a good percentage of the transaction. Thus, I don't need to sell my paintings. I am attached to my work, and as I said, am ready to lend paintings for public or private exhibitions. On rare occasions I trade my work with another artist, if I think that his or her work is of interest to me. But I don't have to sell my paintings to make ends meet. In all likelihood, thinking of selling my work would detract from its quality. This may be an uneasy admission to make, but it's true. I am a firm believer in trading art for its legitimate value, but without being reduced to prostituting it."

Having finished his explanation, Jean-Louis looked at the art collector almost apologetically. The man nodded in understanding, thanked Jean-Louis for his patience and candour and left the café in a pensive mood. Artists are an unpredictable lot, he thought. But at least this one is honest and has a business sense.

Jean-Louis remained seated in the café and ordered a second round of espresso. Thierry, the headwaiter, joined him briefly. They went a long way back, Jean-Louis having been a regular customer for years. He had befriended the faithful waiter, who followed his footsteps and joined the judo club where Jean-Louis practiced, in time becoming a senior pupil.

"What was that all about?" asked Thierry.

"That was an art collector. He seemed a civilised and polite person. The fellow wished to pay me fifty thousand francs for the *Dynamic Nage-Waza* oil painting that I had lent to an exhibition called Art in Sports at the Galleries Bellini. I told him that the painting is not for sale."

"You turned down *cinquante mille francs*?"

"*Oui.*"

"*C'est pas possible!*"

Jean-Louis thought for a moment and answered, "*Les affres de l'esprit tourmenté de l'artiste* (The afflictions of the artist's tormented soul)."

But the disappointed art collector's hunch about Jean-Louis and his business sense had only scratched the surface of the latter's profound business involvement in the world of art. That same weekend, Jean-Louis traveled to his hometown, Belfort, to see his parents. One of his former neighbours told him about an old collection of art photography that was for sale. It turned out that one of the town's established families had decided to clear out the homestead attic. They had found a photo-art collection belonging to a long-deceased great-uncle.

Jean-Louis thanked his neighbour for the lead and telephoned the person charged with disposing of the attic's contents. The ancestor whose collector's items were for sale had had an interest in the earlier forms of photography and had collected daguerreotype plates from the mid-nineteenth century. The silver plates with

Jean-Louis Meets His Match 73

original photos dating back to 1845 had gathered dust in the attic for almost a century, since the great-uncle had acquired them. They definitely qualified as photographic collector's items, but when Jean-Louis cleaned them up and viewed them, his nostrils immediately flared. The half- and quarter-size daguerreotype plates revealed unique artistic quality, with landscapes, portraits and still objects that could not be reproduced. The daguerreotype technique is a quite singular type of art because its chemical imprint on the silver plate is not reproducible by any kind of technology. These had been made by a true master and were probably worth a fortune. The heir, who wished to clear the junk from his attic and sell the plates, clearly had no notion either of their artistic or of their financial worth.

"These are beautiful samples of early photographic art," said Jean-Louis. "What are you expecting to get for them?"

"Oh, I don't really know. Perhaps five thousand francs? Would that be an excessive amount to ask for them, do you think?"

Jean-Louis knew that five thousand francs was about the right price for regular daguerreotype originals. But these were of a different class and the best he had ever seen.

He wrote out a cheque for five thousand francs, saying that he was not in the habit of playing bargaining games with people from his hometown wishing to clear their attics. If he wanted five thousand, five thousand it was.

He packed the plates individually into the luggage compartment of his vehicle. Then he shook hands with the gentleman, who was pleased to see some revenue from his dusty, derelict family storage, and drove off.

Upon returning to Paris, he took the daguerreotypes to the museum's photography curator, who had them assessed. After some negotiation, the museum decided to purchase the unique collection from him, offering one hundred thousand francs. Jean-

Louis agreed, knowing that they might fetch considerably more if privately auctioned. He was happy to make a remarkable profit and yet leave the art on public display at the photography museum.

Following his return from Belfort, he arranged to have a judo training session at the club in the afternoon. He arrived at the martial arts centre, and found in his letter box at the judo club's office a message from the editor of a well-known French geographic magazine. The editor wished Jean-Louis to join him for dinner that evening at 8:00 p.m. in a small, quaint fish restaurant called Le Petit Navire, located near Pont Sully. Jean-Louis left a recording on the editor's answering machine, confirming that he would be at the restaurant at eight, went to the locker room and dressed for practice.

He warmed up on the *tatami* mat for twenty minutes and then worked out with two young second-*dan* black-belt members, practicing *randori* competitor rounds with one referee. Having changed roles several times, he fought at least a dozen rounds and refereed several more; Jean-Louis had coached the two younger men in specific throwing techniques. Despite his build, which was not quite athletic, Jean-Louis moved like a cannonball, with superb speed and agility. He was 1.85 metres tall and weighed slightly over a hundred kilograms. At first sight, he gave the general impression of being a hefty and somewhat cumbersome bespectacled individual, nearly forty years old. But as soon as he trod the judo mat, his whole body worked in perfect unison, with the elegance of a dancer and the driving force of a train engine. The younger *judoka*s, who were muscular, athletic and about fifteen years his juniors, looked like rag dolls compared to Jean-Louis' powerful build.

Practice over, the fellows thanked him for his input and all three headed for the shower room.

Jean-Louis left the club with damp hair under his hat, noting that he had enough time to walk to the restaurant without taking the Métro. He walked along the Boulevard Saint-Germain, enjoying the cool evening breeze after the judo practice and a hot shower.

Le Petit Navire boasted a marine atmosphere in beautiful blue interior décor, with various fishing nets, ship models and brass marine paraphernalia displayed throughout the room. Jean-Louis had built up a healthy appetite, having worked out in the *dojo* and walked for half an hour in the cool Paris evening air. Welcoming his host's suggestion to order dinner first and chat until it was served, he ordered fish soup and a bass fillet to follow. After a glass of eau Perrier and another of Muscadet, the senior editor explained the reason that his magazine wished to buy Jean-Louis dinner in an expensive restaurant.

"We are planning an end-of-the-year special issue to celebrate the coming New Year – 1990 marks a new year and a new decade. The magazine is organising an expedition to the Peruvian Andes. We're in search of authentic and ethnic primitive Andean art. The area we are interested in is the Huaraz district. Some of the small villages in that high-altitude region are hardly accessible by motor vehicle and we will be on muleback for part of this trip. It will be quite an adventure. We are recruiting a highly professional photography team and the best local guides available. But I am offering you to lead this mission. We're looking for the art treasures of Huaraz for our editorial. If you agree to take this assignment and head the expedition, it's likely that you will recognize treasures that another person may not. This assignment has Jean-Louis written all over it. I personally hope that you can take it on, provided that we can reach an adequate agreement, of course."

They had espresso at the end of dinner, and Jean-Louis agreed to consider the offer and contact the editor's office by the end of the following week. Since it was by then almost 11:00 p.m., he decided to go and pick up Annette from her late shift in the surgery clinic. Jean-Louis strolled along the Seine towards the Esplanade des Invalides. He arrived at the surgery a little early; Annette still had latex gloves and an operating-room uniform on.

"Did any interesting work come across your way today, *docteur*?" he inquired.

"I've been stitching like a seamstress all evening. We just had the nightly Parisian quota of wounds and injuries," she answered half seriously.

"Tired?"

"Not too tired. I need to relax a bit and maybe have a drink. Let's do something interesting."

"I was thinking of driving to Les Halles in Rungis to see if the seafood wholesale market can sell us fresh *homard* (lobster). We have guests tomorrow night and I fancy preparing *homard à la thermidor*." They got into Annette's Peugeot and drove to Rungis via Boulevard Périphérique and then the motorway. Les Halles was very active between midnight and the early hours of the morning, taking advantage of the lighter traffic during these hours to deliver huge daily quantities of fresh supplies to Paris's shops and restaurants.

While driving, Jean-Louis told his wife about the dinner and the Peruvian trip offer made by the magazine editor. She loved the idea. "Can I come along?" she asked, sounding like a six-year-old boy unwilling to miss adventure. Jean-Louis mulled over her request for a little while and said, "It's not altogether a bad idea to have a competent physician with a well-kitted emergency bag on an expedition like this one. If I decide to take it on, perhaps I should talk to the editor about you."

The *fruits de mer* wholesaler was delighted to see them. They belonged to a short list of the fish market's most highly esteemed regular guests. He immediately opened a bottle of cold champagne and gave Annette a glass. Jean-Louis returned home well past 2:00 a.m., with bagfuls of freshly caught lobster and a tipsy wife.

Jean-Louis and Annette set out for Lima with the geographic magazine team in early August. The editorial approval committee had promptly authorised Annette's joining the expedition, along with most of Jean-Louis' requests. Thus, everyone was happily on their way. They spent a few days kitting and fitting in beautiful Lima, and then flew to the small Anta airfield near Huaraz with LC Busre, the regional airline. The local guides took charge of driving the rented four-by-four Land Rovers from Lima, and hired a convoy of mules and alpacas for the more difficult and adventurous part of the expedition. They were aiming for the Callejón de Huaylas along the Río Santa riverbed, and the Cordillera Blanca snow-capped mountain ridge.

As the region was known for supplying markets with local artisan crafts, Jean-Louis decided to begin by ransacking the street markets with his photography team. He gleaned all the information that he could from the Huaraz vendors, sometimes at the cost of buying their merchandise or tipping them. He was much more interested in what they had to say regarding their sources than in buying trinkets. His treasures were on film and videotape. He obviously wanted to travel and see where this art was produced and study the local artisans, not only their tourist-marketing apparatus.

The French visitors were greatly affected by what local people term as *soroche*. It is a low-oxygen condition associated with high altitudes, which causes faintness and shortness of breath. *Soroche* affects everyone, but can have a devastating effect on some. Annette was the first to warn against it. She quickly learned from the guides that chewing coca leaves or drinking coca-based maté tea and plenty of water really helps. Notwithstanding these precautions, all foreigners, particularly the indefatigable Jean-Louis, were best advised to take things slow and easy for the first few days in high altitudes.

The expedition set out to the Cordillera mountain ridge looking for workshops, camel-hair weavers, dyes, and poncho, sweater or carpet craftsmen. Jean-Louis also delighted in the *cuarteados* (a typical dessert from the nearby town of Caraz made by mixing *manjar blanco*, a sweet milk-based type of white spread, and fruitcake). He kept the team busy filming and documenting various stages of preparation, and insisted that the locals should help him perfect his skills. The expedition set camp every night anywhere between Huayanca and Chiquián, traveling the mountain ridges in search of landscapes, artisan crafts, stories and special food recipes. The local guides tried to hunt out special items, and Jean-Louis interviewed people, joked, ate and drank with villagers, filming and taping it all. He felt that he was fulfilling his end of the magazine's proposal to the best of his ability.

The great success however, was Annette's involvement with the indigenous population. After she attended to one or two minor injuries, word quickly spread about "*la doctora francesa.*" A few locals would come every night to their camp to seek medical help or advice. She was alert, and pleased to help the needy. She felt somewhat challenged, though, since some of the pathology seen in remote Andean villages was unique to a nonurban environment unpolluted by overmedication and unadulterated by sterile conditions.

One day, the mule-and-alpaca convoy crossed a riverbed pass between two mountain ridges. They were several miles away from any village, but surprisingly, across the pathway there sat an elderly Indian wearing a dark, feathered hat. He had two round-shaped, white alpaca-hair carpets on display. It was not unusual for an artisan to display his goods along a path where he knew some tourists might travel, but that particular man seemed to have been waiting just for them. Having seen hundreds of carpets, ponchos, sweaters and hats over the past weeks, Jean-Louis almost missed the Indian and his two displayed rugs. But somehow, from the corner of his eye, he noticed the white background and the vivid colours. He turned around, stopping the convoy, and studied the two objects carefully. Annette immediately noticed his nostrils flaring.

The hand-printed image on both carpets was an impressive and beautiful expression of warrior heads, in bright red and indigo on a natural white background. The old Indian sat by his work, smoking a clay pipe and observing Jean-Louis carefully. Although he got by with Spanish, mixed with extrapolated French and Latin, Jean-Louis could make no verbal impression on the Indian fellow. One of the local guides came to his aid in the Quechua dialect. The artisan seemed to appreciate and enjoy the interest that Jean-Louis took in his work. The guide was instructed to ask him how much he wanted for the carpets, and the Indian said they were a hundred US dollars a piece. This price was outrageously high for the region. In the Huaraz open-air markets or even in Lima, top-class work of this kind normally retailed for a fraction of that price. Jean-Louis knew that bargaining was part of the game. He made motions of departing without buying and mounted his mule. The Indian was unperturbed, and the convoy continued riding away. But Jean-Louis had a hunch that they would definitely meet the Indian and his carpets again.

Back at the night camp, Jean-Louis instructed the guides to gather more information about the artisan and his work. The elderly man was nicknamed "El Mexicano." He had gained that title due to his unusual quest for refining his artistic skill. He had walked, sailed and hitchhiked all the way to Oaxaca, where the Mexican artisans lived. He had travelled hundreds of miles north to the Pacific coast of southern Mexico. El Mexicano had taken the trouble to travel just in order to learn a textile-dying technique from the locals. This was most unusual for local Andeans who seldom left their native villages. The Oaxaca region is the home of the cochinilla bug, from which cochinilla-red dye is produced. El Mexicano was known for having mastered the technique, bringing his know-how back to the Huaraz region.

Jean-Louis listened carefully to this account and set out to find the Indian the following day, making sure that whatever happened was videotaped. The artisan was waiting at exactly the same spot, on the riverbed in the mountain pass. Jean-Louis shook hands with him and sat down, taking his sketch pad out of his bag. He sketched the Indian, who sat placidly by his two carpets. Having finished his sketch, he gave it to the man, who thanked him effusively. He took the drawing and hid it in his leather bag. Then, Jean-Louis asked the Quechua interpreter to inquire again about buying the carpets. One hundred dollars apiece was the answer he got. Jean-Louis offered fifty. The Indian was unoffended but unwilling. "Sixty dollars," said Jean-Louis, taking the currency out of his wallet and almost handing it to the artisan. The man still shook his head.

Jean-Louis changed tactics. "Ask him how much he is prepared to take if I buy both carpets," he instructed his interpreter. After some lengthy exchange, the interpreter said sheepishly that El Mexicano wanted three hundred dollars for both carpets. At that point, Jean-Louis understood that this was not a bargaining game at all. He took three hundred dollars out of his wallet and handed them over to the Indian.

The man made no move to take the money and remained seated on his haunches, staring pensively at the currency and then at both Jean-Louis and the interpreter. "What does he want now?" Jean-Louis asked with a slight touch of impatience. Again, quite an elaborate verbal exchange in dialect followed. When it ended, the guide seemed baffled and told Jean-Louis: "*El hombre* says that he cannot sell you the carpets. He complains that if he sells you the carpets today, then he will have nothing to do tomorrow."

Jean-Louis calmed down completely. He seemed at peace with that outcome and thanked the old Indian. Then, mounting his mule, he waved good-bye and motioned to the guide to continue the day's journey. Only Annette noticed the pain in his eyes.

Pendejo
1994

Pendejo is the Spanish singular form of *pendejos*, meaning pubic hair. Colloquially, however, this word's semantic use has a variable meaning that depends upon the speaker's location. In Latin America, it is mostly used as a moderately derogatory term. In Mexico specifically, it usually connotes stupidity or awkwardness, describing an obtuse and senseless individual or behaviour. The word is considered profane.

Adelita, a woman of impressive upper-class appearance in her early forties, waited in the consultation area at MD Anderson Cancer Center's oncology department in Houston, Texas. She was expecting to see Dr. Harrison, one of the department's senior specialists. Her beautiful face seemed troubled and strained, and the signs on her skin under her honey-brown complexion bespoke a sleepless night. Accompanied by her younger brother, she had arrived by direct flight from Mexico City a few hours earlier, having scheduled the medical appointment at short notice. The quick telephone-call referral to Dr. Harrison had been made by Dr. Ortega, the renowned US physician's counterpart at the American-British hospital in Tacubaya, Mexico City.

Dr. Harrison beckoned both visitors into his consulting room, and introduced himself. He vaguely recalled his telephone conversation a day earlier with his former pupil Ortega. As far as he remembered from that telephone call, the clinical problem was a primary oesophageal (gullet) tumour.

On the meeting agenda that Harrison's personal assistant had left on his desk, both visitors were registered as "Dr. Fernández." Harrison, a methodical and pedantic person, wished to organise his mind prior to delving into the subject matter. In this case he wondered who was who.

"Which one of you is my patient?" asked Harrison, smiling pleasantly before picking up the medical chart sent from Mexico. He refrained from viewing the chart first, giving personal priority to those who had come to see him.

"I am your patient," said Adelita.

"And I'm her brother, Álvaro Fernández," added her companion, offering his hand to Dr. Harrison.

The oncologist seemed puzzled. "Are you both physicians?" he asked.

Adelita answered promptly, as if well used to fielding this question. "Only Álvaro is a doctor. I'm a PhD in psychology." Her English was fluent and had a singing, graceful Latin-American accent.

But their meeting, all three doctors knew, wasn't aimed at interprofessional or social exchange. The circumstances were serious, and Harrison, an extremely busy person who did not believe in wasting time, soon directed the discussion towards its harsh clinical aspect. He opened the Mexican hospital chart and studied it for a few minutes. Putting aside the file, he said, "The pathology laboratory in Mexico classified the tumour as a squamous cell growth in the tonsil region of your throat. It may be quite invasive, and requires surgical removal. Without surgery, it has a poor prognostic outlook. This type of tumour tends to grow and obstruct both airways and digestive passages.

Moreover, the likelihood of the growth proliferating and invading vital and sensitive organs such as blood vessels is high enough to warrant a surgical therapeutic approach without too much delay or deliberation. The Texas-based institution has extensive experience and better facilities. This is what your doctor in Mexico suggested, and I fully agree with his view."

Harrison succinctly outlined the course of hospital care that she could receive in Houston, answered several clinical questions posed by Dr. Álvaro and then excused himself, apologising about his tight timetable. He left his direct beeper-telephone number with both, promised to be at their disposal at any time or for any reason and disappeared into his ward.

Álvaro had decided to accompany Adelita because he was close to his sister and a physician himself. Now, left in Harrison's office, Álvaro and Adelita discussed the clinical aspects of Harrison's laconic interview. "The surgery itself isn't particularly difficult," said Álvaro. "But it may damage your vocal chords."

"Better a living hoarse toad than a dead canary," responded Adelita with a slightly macabre humour. "He said unequivocally that follow-up treatments depend on some tests he needs to run and the pathology report after excision," she added. "Depending on which, Harrison emphasised that the suggested protocol for prevention may be a little hard on my system."

Álvaro nodded in agreement and said to himself more than to his sister, "That's true. You give yourself no discount from Dr. Harrison's words."

They left the hospital compound in a cab from the taxi queue outside the MD Anderson main lobby. The cab dropped them off at the hotel booked in advance by their travel agent.

Adelita and Álvaro checked into separate single rooms. She urgently needed a rest, and Álvaro badly wanted to smoke. They agreed to meet for dinner and retired to their bedrooms. Álvaro opened the window overlooking a small swimming pool in a colonial-style inner patio. The pool was empty. He took out a soft packet of Mexican Raleigh cigarettes from his inner jacket pocket. Loosening his tie and sitting on a chair in front of the open window, Álvaro wanted to light up but was stopped by a red sign on the hotel room's wall clearly forbidding smoking indoors. "Crazy Gringos," he muttered. He left the room and sat by the pool, lit his Raleigh and inhaled a lungful with gusto. Álvaro had refrained from smoking anywhere near his sister since they had left Mexico City.

His sister, too, had been a heavy smoker until quite recently. In Mexico, Dr. Ortega had been candid with her regarding the probable origin of her throat tumour. The physician had told her that heavy smoking since age fifteen may well have been the growth's primary generator. Smoking coupled with an excessive daily intake of red wine – he was almost certain that these were the reasons triggering malignancy.

Deep inside, Adelita understood that she had lived in denial. While not an alcohol-dependent person by her own definition, she drank socially. Their family belonged to a small, intellectual community of Spanish exiles in Mexico. Her grandparents were republican intellectuals who had fled the civil war and Franco in the 1930s, but remained true to their Spanish way of life. *Vino tinto de mesa* at lunchtime and dinner was part of their culture, and in a way, so was smoking. Ortega, who came from a similar background, understood this problem well; he had witnessed the repercussions of this lifestyle time and again in his practice.

Álvaro, who was a surgeon himself, knew perfectly well that the combination of tobacco and alcohol induced throat cancer. He was obviously sensitive enough not to smoke around his sister at this difficult point of her life, and he reflected on their lifestyle with sadness. What had once appeared to him an almost harmless social habit now seemed a major threat. Having grown up in the sixties and early seventies, he realised that the educated Spanish upper-middle class on the Mexico City and Madrid axis smoked and drank too much. Now, in the mid-nineties, he understood this as a doctor but nonetheless had difficulty in shaking off the socially cultivated habit.

The hotel's limousine service delivered them both to MD Anderson first thing the following morning. At Dr. Harrison's request, Adelita underwent a complete new sequence of scans, blood tests and interviews with the appointed surgeon and anaesthesiologist. An operating-room slot was available for her surgery in two days.

While his sister was undergoing surgery, Álvaro paced outside like a caged lion. He was obviously aware of the risks and even considered donning a uniform and going in. Yet he knew that such behaviour would fall short of acceptable by his fellow surgeon.

Convalescence from the operation took several days, during which Adelita communicated with everyone by using a notepad. She was discharged from the ward and was now waiting for the pathology results and Dr. Harrison's verdict with regard to her follow-up programme. Álvaro rented a car and took advantage of the short break to travel the countryside around Houston, driving his sister around and enjoying the Texas scenery and a choice of local sites and food.

Once all the preparations had been completed, she was summoned for an appointment at Dr. Harrison's office. Álvaro came along with her, and once again they sat in the oncologist's room. The meeting was attended by her surgeon as well. The surgeon explained that all malignancy had been removed from her throat, leaving a clean margin of healthy tissue in her gullet. He also promised Adelita that much of the hoarseness would go away when postsurgical swelling subsided, but a residue of it might remain. During surgery, he had been unable to avoid causing damage to the nerve supply on one side of her vocal chords. Hence, there was some loss of tension in the supporting structures around the chords, but the final change in her speech was yet to be seen. Adelita took this news in her usual stride. She seemed to accept being sentenced to partial hoarseness without surprise or anxiety. "After all, I make a living by prescribing mental-health plans, not singing at the opera" was her response.

Dr. Harrison then took over the lead of the meeting. He recommended a course of chemotherapy followed by radiation therapy. In his opinion, these two preventive measures were essential for keeping the targeted tissues malignancy free. Adelita and Álvaro accepted this without argument. The good news was that the chemotherapy course would only begin in three weeks. Adelita seemed relieved that she could be left alone for some time. Álvaro already felt the strain of nursing an ailing loved one miles away from home. Although supported daily by telephone, both by Adelita's family and his wife, he missed home. Handling the battle against his sister's disease on his own was emotionally difficult. All were aware of the toll that this task exacted. Fortunately, the respite meant that they could travel back to Mexico and say good-bye to MD Anderson and malignancy treatments for twenty days.

Adelita traveled home feeling well, sounding hoarse but radiating optimism. She almost made the ordeal she had been through seem like a holiday with a shopping spree in its final round. She had had the presence of mind to embark on a shopping spree in Montrose prior to departing for the airport. This supplied her with a mountain of presents for her son and two daughters. She even got a handsome leather belt with a silver longhorn buckle for her husband Pablo. Adelita realised that while her spouse was worried over the potential implications of her medical condition, he felt a little left out. He was a Mexican public accountant and his English was poor. There was no hope that he would know his way around an American hospital. Both families had agreed that her brother was obviously a better choice. Álvaro, who had graduated from the medical faculty at the Universidad Nacional de México, later trained as a specialist in one of Boston's best surgery internship programmes. He had obtained American hospital privileges at the time. Clearly, this was an advantage that had influenced the rationale behind the decision of both families to send Álvaro instead of Pablo to Houston.

Home again without a sick sister to look after, Álvaro went back to full-time work. Although his two associates had handled things smoothly and efficiently, he felt that he needed to work. Getting away from tumours had been surprisingly refreshing, even after almost fifteen years of practice. His wife and son required much of his time as well, even if his own small family seemed to handle this abrupt change in routine. But the only remark that marred this idyllic situation came from his wife. "Álvaro, why are you smoking so much since you came back from Texas?"

He could find no good answer to this question. Trying to rationally answer it defied common sense, regardless of the circumstances.

Back in Houston three weeks later, Adelita was scheduled to begin her chemotherapy course. This time, instead of staying at the hotel they rented a small apartment at a tidy residential complex in Braeswood called the English Inn. During the four weeks of the therapy course, Adelita attended a weekly session at Dr. Harrison's day care clinic. The day after her first treatment she felt horrid. She had no energy, suffered from bouts of unbearable nausea and developed facial-skin dryness and other unpleasant side effects. This lasted for nearly three days, gradually wearing off until reaching a normal state. To make it easier to bear,

Adelita was given an explanatory booklet written by the oncology department's social service team. I'm being fed some of my own medicine, she thought to herself.

After the first round of chemotherapy, Álvaro suggested that she consult the department's doctor, who specialised in palliative care aimed at helping those who suffered from the therapy's side effects. The doctor recommended herbal medication developed in France and claimed that some outpatients had reported successful results. This seemed worth exploring, and the intervention proved beneficial. The use of the herbal formula following her second session of chemotherapy considerably reduced the nausea and also shortened the fatigue spells. The improvement had provided Adelita with more bearable interim spells between the weekly intravenous sessions. Suffering seemed to downsize itself.

She disliked attending the clinic, getting an inevitable blood test to monitor cell counts before each session, waiting for her turn in the therapy area along with other sick persons receiving their weekly dosage and staying put for two hours with an intravenous fluid drip stuck in her forearm. She put up with it because she wanted to live, and it was obviously the right thing to do. But Adelita wished to put this episode behind her and felt anxiety creeping up on her whenever she went near the day care corridor. There was a healthy refusal in her to become part of a sick milieu. During the intravenous treatment sessions, all Álvaro could do was hold her hand and chat to her, or be silent – whichever she preferred.

When tired of being part of a world full of cancer, Álvaro made use of an outdoor pool, spent time in the laundry room, or sat in his room and smoked two or three cigarettes in a row. He still refrained from smoking in his sister's presence, and had to compensate for it. Whenever he thought about how harmful cigarettes were, he put it out of his mind. "Not now," he reasoned, trying to convince himself that "later" was all the time in the world to quit.

Radiation therapy immediately followed, with daily sessions in the radium unit on the sub-basement floor. Located in the bowels of the medical centre, this establishment enjoyed relative quiet compared to the busy day care clinic. But not only the alien machinery and chilling metallic names such as "cobalt" and "radiation units" (rads) put Adelita through misery. The accumulated effect of potent radiation on the tissues of her swallowing mechanism caused havoc. Early on in the radiation treatment course, Adelita developed throat swelling and severe discomfort. She was unable to take in solid food and was limited to fluid nutrition. Her gullet felt as if someone had used it instead of a smoke pit.

Adelita's body, still hard hit and trying to overcome the massive poisoning caused by chemotherapy, could hardly stand the daily burning. She cried every time Álvaro drove her to MD Anderson, and cried all the way back. For the first time during the whole fight, she really felt that her grip on the situation was slipping away. Álvaro had alerted Dr. Harrison about this development and an ear, nose and throat specialist was immediately brought into the picture, in an attempt to save the day. Radiotherapy was stopped for twenty-four hours and some medication was administered to relax the insulted tissues.

Álvaro assessed the situation and rang up Mexico City, asking Pablo to come and spend the weekend with his wife. This boosted Adelita's spirits and afforded Álvaro some free time, which he used for going on a short fishing trip near Galveston. This last round of therapy proved to be the toughest. Adelita's physical and mental strength were being tested to their limit, and so was Álvaro's endurance. But they were nearing the final laps, and determined to win. When not in therapy, Adelita rested in the rented apartment. She was unable to eat effectively, weakened by the intense attack on her body and on her mind. But she counted days and rads, and hoped for the best.

Álvaro sat outside Dr. Harrison's office, waiting to briefly see him regarding some test results needed for assessment. Adelita was attending therapy and would be through in an hour. Across the corridor from him stood a magnificent-looking giant of a man with deep brown skin who wore his jet black hair in a short ponytail. By looks and attire, he was of American Indian origin. The man seemed stressed out; his shoulders shook and his eyes were red. Álvaro had seen him at the ward on several occasions, but had never spoken to him. Approaching the Indian, he put his hand on his arm and softly asked, "What's up, are you all right?"

The Indian answered: "Doc said that I got cancer in my liver, in my brain and in my bones now."

"Can he do anything about it?" asked Álvaro.

"Doc said they already did all they could." He took out a handkerchief, cleared his nose and coughed. He had obviously been trying to stifle a sob. "They took out a chunk of my lungs before Christmas two years ago," he added. "Then they kept me here and gave me medication through the veins, enough to kill a horse with. It took more than a year to grow my hair back on again. But doc said I'll be OK and I went right back to work on scaffoldings, see?" As proof, he showed Álvaro both his palms.

"Now, doc tells me that I got growths in the liver and brain, and more in my bones. They tried, but can't stop them growths with drip bags into the veins, or radiation machine anymore. They can't hack them out either."

"I see" said Álvaro. "How old are you?"

"I'm only fifty-two years old," answered the Indian. "And I quit smoking over two years ago, as soon as they found the cancer. But doc said it was too late, too damn late."

He burst out crying and his huge shoulders racked and shook in sobs. Álvaro just stood by him, keeping his hand between the big man's shoulder blades. After a while the man's crying subsided and he settled down. Álvaro left silently and went to look for his sister. The encounter with the Indian had shocked him. It had drained him of energy, and all he wanted to do was to go home and relax. The image of a huge, tough man reduced to sobs and the words "too damn late" would not leave him.

Once back in their apartment, Adelita retired to her bedroom. She was pale and tired after therapy, her throat burned and she said that she needed to lie down and be left alone. Álvaro went into his bedroom and lit a Raleigh. The ashtray in his room was full of cigarette ends, and the room smelled of stale smoke. He opened the window to let in fresh air and sat in front of the open window, smoking and thinking.

When the burning end of his cigarette nearly reached the filter mouthpiece, he put it out in the ashtray. The crying Indian lived vividly in his mind. He could not close his eyes without seeing the huge man, with dark skin and ponytail, crying. Álvaro emptied the ashtray's contents into a wastepaper basket. He opened the cupboard where he kept the carton of Raleigh cigarettes brought from Mexico, took out the remaining packets, added the open one from his shirt pocket and threw them all into the dustbin. Then he carried the wastebasket to the yard and emptied it out into the refuse disposal. Purge completed, he went back to the apartment and stood by the mirror. Looking at himself but seeing the Indian, he vowed: "*Por pendejo, yo no voy a morir.*"

Freely translated into English, this means: "I won't die for being a *pendejo*."

Barracuda Reef
1995

Tom Travis worked his way through medical school under water. His summer breaks were spent working on oil rigs in the ocean, or doing underwater salvage in the North Sea. Even guiding scuba safaris in the Caribbean was fine, if the money was right. During semester holidays Tom sometimes spent time cleaning barnacle off ship hulls in the nearby harbour. That was a nasty but well-paid job because such a task in commercial dock waters was usually filthy and cold, and demanded diving in a dry suit.

Thus Tom managed to earn a living by literally keeping his nose just above water throughout his medical training. He even continued now and again to use his underwater expertise and skills when specialising in physical medicine after receiving his degree, thereby supplementing his modest income as a resident.

Upon finalising his specialised training, it was natural for him to take the time to add a course in diving medicine to his curriculum. After all, he had witnessed it all first hand. In Tom's case, the underwater environment, physiology and perils of hyperbaric injury or other diving risks were not only theoretically acquired knowledge, but second nature. By that time, scuba and its related diving-medicine sideline had comfortably become leisure pastimes rather than breadwinning pursuits.

Every summer Professor Stein, the head of the marine biology interuniversity laboratory, invited Tom to come and teach the university's research students a short course on scuba-related injuries and health risks. Knowing the essentials of preventing decompression disease and other dangers was crucial to the students' safety. The marine lab was located on the southern coast next to a tropical sea, and its research centre carried out many projects involving underwater tasks. The majority of the research students had no previous scuba experience. They underwent a basic training course in diving before their semester began. After they qualified as divers, their divemaster allocated two full course days for Tom's input.

Tom considered his lessons to be very important, since researchers were prone to forget themselves while engrossed in scientific work. Incidents in which safety rules were overlooked for the sake of adrenalin-charged research thrills were not unheard of. Tom upheld safe diving and habitually began his class by presenting the following slide:

**It's no crime if you don't dive by the book.
But it may carry a death penalty.**

In the summer of 1995 the marine biology research centre invited Tom down to lecture before their MSc students. The institution paid for his airfare and a suite of rooms at the diving centre's hotel. He was their honorary guest for the week. It was his fifth summer teaching the injury-prevention programme, and Tom was thrilled to be participating. His arrangement with the university gave him an opportunity to be underwater in a colourful tropical sea, get away from his clinical work for a few days and spend time with an academic crowd. He loved diving and the submarine realm, in spite of all the years spent working in cold murky waters. Bright young minds that looked up to him were a tonic. Tom enjoyed it tremendously, over and above the prospect of being underwater and his addictive diver's need for breathing compressed air.

On the first morning of his two-day schedule, Tom showed up at the dive counter where scuba gear was checked out for his students. He required some props for his lecture, and was delighted to see Leah Silver's familiar face behind the counter. She had been a pupil in the previous year's cohort and one of the most academically impressive persons in that crowd. Presently she was in the process of wrapping up her research project. Leah's family lived locally. Since she was a longtime divemaster in her own right, the university's full-time divemaster had offered her a summer job. Her duties were to help out with the diving plans for new students, look after scuba equipment and manage the compressor room. Last summer, she had spent time with Tom building up her underwater research platform. Benefiting from his vast experience, Leah regarded Tom as her submarine mentor, second in command only to Neptune.

Tom checked out a steel air cylinder, a regulator with an extra second stage (an additional breathing intake unit, also called an "octopus"), a mask with a snorkel, a neoprene suit and a pair of fins. While laying out the gear for him, Leah asked, "Planning any adventurous dives while down here with us, doctor?"

"I'll probably dive, but I've brought my own equipment. This gear is for my first lecture. I'll be here for another few days after teaching, just for diving. But maybe we can grab a bite in the evening and I'll discuss my diving plans with you. You can also update me on your research project."

Leah beamed. She liked Tom and found the prospect of catching up with him exciting. "Sure. Let's get something to eat after your teaching is over today. I'll still be behind the counter when today's lecture schedule ends. Check with me on your way out."

Tom carefully balanced the equipment on a metal trolley and wheeled it towards the lecture room. He spread out the gear on the desk near the slide projector and placed small cardboard signs by each piece. The labels were peculiarly worded with the terms "Hypothermia," "CO_2 buildup," "Air contamination" and the like. This was his party piece to be enjoyed today. He looked forward to it.

The group of curious marine biologists took seats in the small lecture theatre and Tom's day began. After a short introduction, he picked up a scuba mask and asked, "Everyone knows what this is for?"

All nodded unanimously in agreement. "Now you will learn how in a worst-case scenario, when improperly used a simple mask like this can drown you…"

Leah left the counter a while after Tom checked out, after making sure that no one required her help. She stepped into the small glass cubicle office at the back of the equipment room and made a telephone call to a girlfriend who knew Tom. Her friend taught in a school near the hospital where Tom practiced. After all, like all reef dwellers she needed to develop strong survival skills and be open-eyed and cautious when important matters of this nature cropped up.

Her friend had made some discreet inquiries through the hospital grapevine and had a full report ready for Leah: "Tom is still single and at this time seems to be in great demand among our neighbourhood women. He was inseparable from Margaret, a very attractive young internist, for a long time up until this winter. After Christmas she was offered a better job and relocated to a hospital in another city, trading Tom for a better position and a bigger pay cheque. Their relationship didn't endure the separation and dwindled after a couple of months of love shuttling across the country. He was heartbroken for some time but recently has begun dating here and there. No woman had succeeded in making his eyes shine yet. If he's on your turf now, I wish you good luck."

Leah seemed pleased with her friend's inquiry results. She telephoned her favourite Thai restaurant in town and reserved a table for that evening.

"Ladies and gentlemen," said Tom, moving into his concluding remarks for the day. "Faulty equipment – usually due to poor upkeep, bad underwater habits and oversight as well as bad luck – are the reasons for diving accidents. Statistics tell us that in 99 percent of accidents, negligent equipment maintenance and diving 'not by the book' are the culprits, with bad luck serving only as a complicating factor. Never blame just bad luck. That is today's tip. Tomorrow, we will spend time learning about underlying pathology as a potential risk in diving. Whether overt or covert, health-related conditions can expose us to diving sickness. Good evening to all of you."

Tom trolleyed the scuba equipment back to the counter and checked it in with Leah. Before he set out to go back to the hotel, she asked, "Is Thai food all right with you for tonight?" Tom said it was.

She gave him a note with the restaurant's name and address. "It's a five-minute walk from your hotel. I'll bring my research file along and meet you there at eight o'clock."

The Thai restaurant had a beautiful pagoda-like entrance, making it conspicuous and easy to find. Tom arrived a few minutes early and was led to the table that Leah had reserved. He ordered a drink while waiting for her. As she came through the glass door he realised for the first time what a classically beautiful woman she was. In his mind's eye, her image had been that of a compressor-room operator wearing grease-stained overalls, noise-protecting earmuffs and a soiled T-shirt. His visual memory of her from the previous summer had been obliterated by time, Margaret and an ethical, hermetically sealed ban on fraternising with his students. Now, he saw an elegant, long-legged young lady in a simple but attractive black dress. She was wearing a thin white silk scarf and tiny diamond earrings. Although not overly ornate, she had clearly dressed for the hunt.

Tom had naïvely thought that his suggestion in the morning to catch up with her at night had had no underlying romantic motive. On second thought, he wondered whether deeper insight had failed to spell out the true drive for their meeting. By the time she sat down, he had come to grasp that she was two steps ahead of the game. Tom was pleased.

They had dinner, split a bottle of wine and the bill and discussed her research project in depth. Tom made a few technical comments on her final underwater protocol and was happy to be just her friendly advisor rather than her appointed tutor. They left the restaurant by ten o'clock and took a walk along the seafront. On returning to town Leah looked for a cab. "Let's get the hotel to order a taxi for you," Tom suggested. A cruising cab pulled up to the hotel driveway as they approached the entrance and Tom hailed it.

"See you at the lab tomorrow," Tom called as Leah got into the taxi.

Leah smiled. "I'll be there tomorrow morning. But consider me for some serious diving when you're done teaching. I'm fed up with novice divers in need of an underwater nanny."

"Deal done!" replied Tom. For the first time in a while he felt excited.

The following day was spent teaching diving medicine and its practical implications. Researchers doing underwater work on their projects needed to be aware of these risks. The workload differed somewhat from recreational scuba diving and required a tougher safety approach. Tom had the advantage of having done the walk. The lab director ordered all his staff to attend these lectures, not only the student body. Leah sat in on some of the lectures, when she wasn't needed in the compressor room. When Tom finished his teaching session, he went over to her counter.

She was busy filling up air tanks, and he waited until the compressor noise was cut off to talk to her.

"We have a faculty dinner tonight. I'll be here midmorning tomorrow as your lab director's guest, to take a look at facility developments during this past year. My friend Adam, a veteran navy diver, is flying in and I plan to do some diving with him. Maybe you could join us when you're off work."

Leah nodded in agreement and Tom added, "But the faculty dinner will be over by about nine thirty. Find us a quiet bar or somewhere pleasant to sit and have a drink. I could be there by ten o'clock."

"Blue Lagoon at ten o'clock is good. It's on the northbound road a few miles out of town, overlooking the bay. They have a good selection of quiet music. I'll try to steal one of our family cars. Take a cab out and I'll drive us back." Tom wrote "Blue Lagoon" on his notepad and left Leah to her compressor.

The Blue Lagoon had a great bay view and an impressive choice of brandy. The town and harbour lights reflected in the ocean, forming a quiet, faraway picture. Tom sipped his brandy and asked, "Have you always lived here?"

"Since I was six years old," replied Leah. "My dad was contracted to build part of the harbour. He is a civil engineer and runs his own construction firm. We've been living here for over twenty years. It's been a little strange living at home again since I began the MSc marine biology programme. I'd been away from home for almost five years before that, between university and working up north. Now, I'm daddy's little girl again." She smiled. "Although I live in the house annex and have my own independent life, my dad tends to forget that I'm a big girl now and has reverted to treating me like a teenager all over again. My mom is much more sensible about my return home and, in fact, sometimes saves him from embarrassment."

Tom took in her exposé and asked, "Where will you go from here?"

"With the exception of some minor additions and corrections, my appointed tutor approved the MSc dissertation for submission in September. It means that my term here at the lab will be over in a few weeks. I guess the sky is the limit then. I've already started job hunting. Options vary between biotechnological marine agriculture to training centres for marine mammals. I could end up working anywhere."

When they finished their drinks, Tom and Leah drove back to town and parked by the beach. Tom took off his shoes and rolled his trousers to knee level to stroll in the waterline's wet sandy end. Leah kicked off her sandals and joined him, taking his hand. It was past midnight when she dropped him off at the hotel.

She was pleased that he had sought her company after the faculty event. Intuitively she sensed that he was sophisticated but totally lacked suavity. She felt that Tom would abide by the laws of nature and would not be easy to domesticate. The ocean waves and mountain winds were to govern his life. She was intrigued by this feeling, but not deterred.

Back in his suite, Tom sprawled on the couch in front of the television set and searched for the following day's weather forecast. The outlook for scuba was good. He turned off the television and lay on his back, thinking. Leah was bright, attractive and obviously interested. Although he was ten years her senior, this difference seemed natural and never cropped up as an issue. It didn't seem to be an obstacle at all. Nonetheless, for him it spelled caution. He had spent three years in a relationship that was ultimately given up for a job. Regardless of age, Tom had neither the wish nor the time to repeat this mistake. Although not overly emotional by nature, he realised that he had been hurt. His career was going well where he was, and he saw prospective advance and promotion as well as professional interest. There would be no reason to consider any relocation for the foreseeable future. Could Leah fit in, or did their budding relationship harbour the risk of yet another potential sacrifice – love for career?

What the hell, he told himself just before falling asleep. Let's start by taking her diving tomorrow.

It was Friday morning and Tom paid a visit to the hospital, catching up with old acquaintances and visiting the newly refurbished pressure chamber. It was run by an old friend who had taught as part of the team in Tom's diving-medicine specialty course. They spent a short while reminiscing on old divers' tales. Afterwards Tom went to meet Adam, his diving buddy, at the airport. They took a taxi to the hotel. After Adam checked in they went together to the marine biology lab. On the way, Tom filled Adam in on their potential diving partner. "It's about time you got over Maggie, old boy. This new woman sounds like just the right medicine for your sickness."

"How the hell would you know? You've never seen her," answered Tom. But they both knew that he wasn't insulted. Tom was just keeping up their old joust. Adam was known for having a kind heart which cohabited in disharmony with a wild mind. He was a highly professional and experienced diver. The two friends shared a nearly twenty-year underwater history and Tom couldn't remember missing an opportunity for having a go at each other.

They arranged to visit the oceanic lab facilities with the director, who was a professor of marine biology. The director proudly pointed out that much of the new equipment had been introduced over the past few months at Tom's advice. He volunteered local diving site information regarding places that Tom and Adam were looking forward to exploring that weekend. He also lent Tom one of the lab's pick-up trucks for driving to the sites and lugging their diving gear about.

After the marine biologist had gone back to his duties, Tom and Adam came by the dive counter to look for Leah.

She was busy servicing diving equipment and stopped for a moment when Tom introduced Adam.

"Professor Stein told us about a nearby shallow site called Barracuda Reef, where a beautiful school of fair-sized barracudas have recently been spotted every day at sunset. If your timetable allows a dive this evening, perhaps we could meet you when you finish your shift and set out from here?"

"Perfect," answered Leah. "I'll get a nightlight charged and my equipment ready for five o'clock. By the time we get to the site and kit up it will be dusk. I'm due at my parents' for dinner at eight o'clock, so we'll have just enough time."

Tom and Adam drove back to the hotel, grabbed a sandwich and went over their diving gear. They relied on Leah's counter for their air cylinders and lead weights, but got all the rest ready and loaded on their truck. By a quarter to five they were back at the lab and waiting for her to close up.

The offshore reef was about twenty minutes away on the southbound road, and they parked the truck a short distance away from the waterline. Adam carried one nightlight, and Leah gave Tom the light she had charged. Both lights worked well. All three divers finned on their backs for about a hundred metres until they were hovering over the reef, which was six to eight metres deep and marked with a buoy. They released the air from the buoyancy vests and sank on the reef's edge.

Sunset still provided enough daylight not to require artificial light. They swam underwater in a straight line, with Leah in the middle. Well-trained divers, they quietly glided through the water with perfect buoyancy and balance. In the warm water the dive was silky and magical. When the sunlight vanished, the evening grew more intimate. Twilight turned into darkness and the phosphorescent sea life glowed luminously. The divers swam slowly along the reef, searching for underwater life as the dusk deepened around them.

About fifteen minutes into the dive, a shining silver school of barracudas majestically appeared just above a rock at a depth of seven metres. Tom and Adam turned their lights on. At first the fish didn't move much, but suddenly all shifted in unison, reflecting light in a mesmerising mirror-like effect. The divers kept swimming around the reef to complete a full circle. On the way, they occasionally met a lionfish or giant moray eel.

Having swum three-quarters of the reef's circumference, Leah signaled to Tom that something was wrong. She pointed to her head and made hand signals indicating a problem. Tom tried to catch Adam's attention but the latter was a little too far to the right, busy shining his light on a large black-fin barracuda which he had spotted. He took no notice of his diving buddies. Tom attempted to flash his light at Adam, making fast movements with the beam to alert him. Unfortunately, Leah's light had become weak. Instead of a long bright white beam, it emitted a yellowish-orange shine that barely illuminated a few inches around it. It went unnoticed at a distance, so Tom gave up trying to draw Adam's attention.

Leah appeared sallow, distressed and in need of Tom's full focus. The immediate danger was her passing out underwater and drowning. Tom performed a controlled rescue procedure, discarding her weight belt first, surfacing and at the same time keeping Leah's regulator firmly in her mouth to make sure that she breathed air and not water. Hitting the surface, he inflated both vests, and unbuckled and dropped his own lead belt. He took the regulator out of Leah's mouth. She was conscious but said that she felt dizzy and had a terrible headache.

Since there was still no sign of Adam, Tom began towing Leah inshore. She was lying on the water flat on her back. By the time he reached shallow water and could get a better grip on things he saw Adam's light at a distance flickering above water. Tom thought about waiting for Adam but he was concerned about Leah, who looked pale and sick. He assumed that Adam, now above water, would have no trouble.

Tom wanted to get Leah onto dry land and tried to shine the light, looking for a comfortable sandy stretch to beach her on. However, the light was almost completely out, weaker than a small candle. He switched it off and felt the rocky seabed with his hands in order to grasp Leah's shoulders. At this point he couldn't really see where his hands touched and he accidentally leaned on a long-spine black sea urchin. His left hand was stung by the puncturing spines. Leah's condition being the priority, Tom ignored his minor injury. He landed her on the sandy shore and pulled off her vest and air cylinder, leaving only the wet suit. Her pulse was quick and her skin warm and a little dry. He immediately thought of dehydration. The truck was nearby and he ran to fetch a bottle of mineral water. She drank a mouthful and immediately vomited it.

Adam had found the discarded lead belts when still underwater and gathered that an emergency situation had cropped up. He caught up with them on the beach. As he approached, Tom dryly reported: "She's dehydrated and urgently needs fluids. Her digestive tract is in shock and she is unable to absorb water. Let's get her to the hospital. You drive." They placed Leah on her back in the rear seat and piled all the diving gear into the truck. Adam got behind the wheel and they drove off. Tom sat next to Leah and wetted her lips with a soaked clean towel. She was awake, but confused and quiet.

The emergency room admitted Leah promptly. She was put in a cubicle and examined by the attending physician, who was surprised to see Tom in a scuba suit. "Dr. Travis, we haven't seen you here dressed quite like this before," he said. He noticed the slight bleeding marks and swelling on Tom's left hand and asked about it. "Never mind that," answered Tom. "Just get saline into her vein as soon as you can."

Leah was given a large quantity of fluids intravenously. The relieving effect was nearly immediate. She regained clarity quickly. Still pale and weak, she spoke coherently and asked Tom to call her home. "I was due back home at eight o'clock for dinner," she said. "Ring my parents, tell them where I am and ask them to come."

Tom used the telephone in the nurse's station and dialed the number that Leah had given him. Her dad answered the call.

"Tom Travis speaking. I'm Leah's friend. She felt sick after diving and we've had to bring her to the hospital to give her first aid. She's all right now and wants you to come. Please bring some dry clothes for her." Leah's father said that he would be there shortly.

Tom returned to Leah's side a moment before the attending physician walked towards them. The doctor told them that except for lack of fluids and increased blood tonicity, Leah was fine. He pointed out, however, that the hospital computer records showed that she had attended the hospital's outpatient clinic earlier that week and had been diagnosed with a urinary tract infection. The clinic had prescribed an antibiotic course of treatment for her.

Sitting by Leah's bedside, Tom took stock of the situation.

He had a diving accident on his hands and felt personally guilty not only as a professional diver and physician, but also as Leah's friend. Obviously, she had spent all day inside the hot compressor room and hadn't drunk enough. She had probably started out her dive in partial dehydration. He might have foreseen that before diving and advised her to drink a few glasses of water, but had neglected to do so. The underlying urinary tract infection might well have compromised her body's fluid balance, possibly causing liquid loss and body salts imbalance. Tom couldn't be held responsible for this unreported condition, yet he felt that he had failed her, that he should have been more alert.

They were very lucky to have ventured just a shallow dive. In greater depth, her physiology would have been exposed to a higher pressure. The accident could have had a severe or even fatal outcome. To add insult to injury, equipment malfunction and poor diver discipline had further complicated matters. His trusted longtime dive buddy had negligently lost eye contact with them underwater during a night dive. That had been a serious failure. Both errors had somewhat affected how he dealt with Leah's condition, but had mainly resulted in his hand injury. That could have been avoided had Adam been on the spot with his light working. Fortunately, sea-urchin spine puncture is a bothersome but not dangerous injury. An unlucky sting by a poisonous species could have had far worse consequences. The complete scenario made Tom feel foolish and professionally inadequate.

Leah's father hurried in. He seemed stressed and rushed into her curtained compartment, where Tom was sitting. Leah was still weak, but improving. The attending doctor had told both Tom and her father that all being well, emergency would release her in about an hour.

To Tom's dismay, Leah's father had barely set eyes on his sick daughter when he immediately started yelling at her: "Do you realise that you've ruined our Friday night dinner? We were all waiting for you to come home and where do you end up? In the emergency room! Do you call yourself a responsible adult person?"

Tom was shocked. Before Leah's father went any further, he put his hand on the man's shoulder and said placidly, "Mr. Silver, can I have a word with you outside, please?" He practically pushed her father out of the cubicle and actively escorted him out of the emergency area. Once outside, he looked Mr. Silver directly in the eyes and said, "Your daughter is very weak at this time and has been through a serious threat to her wellbeing. She's OK but is still recovering from shock. Right now, she needs love and support. Please don't tell her off. All she expects you to do is give her a hug and be there for her."

Tom felt like hitting Silver but he spoke as quietly and gently as he could. However, his face had become dark and stern. His eyes glowed with angry sparks. Mr. Silver felt the radiating intensity of Tom's wrath, but also noticed his deep caring. He was visibly taken aback by Tom's stance and sheepishly went into Leah's cubicle to apologise and hug her.

The emergency-room physician in charge gave Leah a discharge letter and said that she could go home. Tom came in to help her get dressed. Colour had returned to her face, and she seemed happy.

"Your father is some man," Tom told her.

"Funny that you should say so," replied Leah. "He said exactly the same about you." She held his hand, squeezed it gently and added, "Welcome to our family."

A Reasonable Person
2003

Captain (Res.) Isaac wiped away the frothy moustache left by the foam head of his beer. He curiously eyed the meticulously uniformed female lieutenant colonel sitting across the table from him. The look in his eyes reflected amusement and respect, while his body language expressed personal sympathy. Their convergence seemed natural and almost well rehearsed.

"How have you been, Isaac?"

"Well, as you know I retired from the force last year. Twenty years of service were enough. At thirty-eight, with nearly 70 percent of my pension rights, it seemed a good time for me to embark on a civilian career. I was offered a partnership in a security firm that offers anti-terror training supervised by the Israeli government. We provide services to friendly nations in Europe, the ex-Soviet block and sometimes Central America. I'm now a legalised broker for mercenary services, if you like," Isaac said with a wink. "But basically, I'm still a soldier. It's hard to shake off the habit. Despite being a father of three, a civilian and a director of a company, I am what I am. You've lived around me and my team long enough to know what we're made of." The woman nodded in agreement.

"But enough about me. What have you been up to, Yael?"

Lieutenant Colonel Levy took in his succinct report, thought for a moment and replied, "Last year, around the time you retired, I was promoted from legal advisor to central command, to the post of senior military-court judge. In my present position I oversee disciplinary action at the military level. I decide whether some cases will be dealt with at the procedural hearing level, or whether punitive action should be taken. At times, a case may even be sent as far as criminal court-martial." She paused and smiled. "I'm on the side of the bad guys now." Pointing to her new shoulder insignia, she added, "They threw this fancy rank into the bargain too."

"The title of judge and the rank become you," said Isaac with a broad, white-toothed grin. "You're by far the prettiest lieutenant colonel here today." She crossed her legs and her eyes twinkled at his compliment.

"Don't forget that I'm almost old enough to be your older sister," she said with a hint of shyness and then added, "You yourself don't look too bad. You seem to have lost some muscle bulk, but not replaced it with fat."

"All true," replied Isaac, who had been mindful of the changes in his career demands and had sought the help of his former physical training officer to devise an appropriate programme for his present status.

"But surely, you haven't summoned me here today just to make certain that I didn't retire into rolls of fat. To what might I owe the honour of your buying my beer?"

"I need your learned opinion regarding a legal matter that I have to deal with now," replied Yael.

Isaac nearly choked on his beer, making an effort to avoid siphoning out some of it through his nose. Once his windpipe and throat settled down, he eyed his hostess quizzically. "Funny. That's like Mike Tyson asking the neighbourhood sports coach for international boxing-match advice."

"Not quite," answered the woman. She pulled out a thick file from a manila envelope. Its cardboard cover was marked "Top Secret." Below the security classification line there was a serial number, and then a title: "Hebron Brigade. Operation Beit Dahar, Feb. 3, 2002."

"I recall this action, but know relatively little about the event," said Isaac. "I was on my retirement vacation at the time, and took no part whatsoever in that particular operation."

She calmly replied, "That's exactly why I need you to look at it. You're objective. But that's not the only reason. Your experience is beyond comparison with anyone else's. You worked yourself up through the ranks, in the same outfit – from soldier, then to sergeant and to officer. Your record shows nearly three times more relevant operational activity and field work than any other career or reserve officer. You were one of the toughest, but always the fairest. I witnessed a large part of your active years. I obtained senior command authorisation to consult with you as a professional advisor. The case is a complex procedural and legal one, and involves a moral dilemma. It needs to be addressed sensibly and precisely, and I need your input."

"Well, before I get a swollen head, you know that I'm but a soldier. I have a simple, practical mind and definitely not a scholarly one." Isaac paused to take a sip of his beer. "Legal moral issues can escape my attention by more than a mark," he added. "What exactly would you like me to do about this file?"

"Read it in your spare time. Try to go through it within a few days. Don't leave it unattended; lock it up when not reading it. Ring me when you're done. My driver will pick it up from your office or home. Then we can meet again and discuss it."

Isaac agreed to take a look, curious as to what he was getting himself into. After a few more minutes of conversation, he drank up the remains of his beer, got up and gave Yael a peck on each cheek. He collected the manila file from the table and left.

The Beit Dahar file proved to be interesting reading. The thick dossier contained various reports. The first one was an assessment report that came from military intelligence. It was signed by a senior officer and dealt with field intelligence information, compiled and obtained in both the Hebron district and in northeast Lebanon. Annexed to this part of the file was a report written by a GSS (General Security Service) intelligence evaluation specialist in Jerusalem. All the documents referred to the Toukan brothers, members of a clan (*hamullah*) residing in Beit Dahar. The elder brother, Ibrahim, aged twenty-three, had served several short jail terms for vehicle theft and house burglary. Prison authorities reported that he had been recruited and sworn into a terrorist group while in prison. He had also been previously employed by an Israeli house-gardening firm in Jerusalem. Therefore, Ibrahim had connections with several Israeli residents who, unaware of his background, would innocently request his gardening services from time to time.

The more interesting information, however, came from Lebanon. Some high-resolution photography spotted Ibrahim in a training camp run by Hezbollah in the depth of the country, near the Syrian border. Ibrahim was reported to have had three months of small arms and explosives training.

The younger Toukan brother, aged nineteen, was named Rafik and had matriculated from a secondary school in Bethlehem. He had no prison record. Recently he had become deeply religious, and now wore a beard and a white cap. His days were spent mostly at home and at the mosque. Intelligence suggested that he belonged to a radical Islamic religious sect. Possibly, Rafik was involved in attempts to recruit impressionable youngsters who would be good candidates for suicide-bombing missions (*shahid*s).

The officer in charge of that part of the investigation file recommended that the two brothers be picked up for questioning as soon as such an operation could be mounted. His assessment clearly indicated that the two were potentially dangerous and were able and equipped to generate an act of terrorism. "Ticking time bombs" was the term he had used.

The Hebron brigade command authorised the suggested operation, seconded it to the special border police SWAT (Special Weapons and Tactics) team and gave it priority and an OK for action. The SWAT team chosen and thus subjected to military-command authority was led by twenty-seven-year-old Lieutenant O.

The second part of the file that Isaac read consisted of the operation's de-briefing reports, written, as a matter of routine, in the wake of the action's aftermath.

Lieutenant O's debriefing was the most comprehensive, as would stand to reason since he had commanded the operation. He briefly mentioned the background and intelligence report, which he had read before setting out to prepare for the action. The SWAT unit operations office had very precise and updated satellite photos of the Toukan house. They also had detailed information regarding the two brothers' schedule. There was every indication that both would be present at the family house on the night of February 3. A virtual computer model of the house was built from information collected by field agents. It had been cross-checked with local collaborators and assumed to be 100 percent accurate. O and his team knew exactly who inhabited each room and where they slept, as well as the exact location of every obstacle, water tank and corridor or stairway passage in the three-storey structure. It was also assumed that weapons and ammunition or an explosive stash lurked somewhere.

O's operational concept was that everything would be over

long before the stash could be accessed. The plan was to attack in complete surprise, gain full control of everyone within the house, seize the two brothers and make a clean exit within three minutes of arrival at the premises.

The night chosen for action was forecasted as cold and stormy. This uninviting setting was perfect, considerably reducing the likelihood of involving innocent bystanders at 2:00 a.m.

O's team had practiced the complete routine dozens of times on a mock-up, studied the entry and exit routes and worked out a plan that would be as foolproof as possible under such constraining circumstances. A parachute brigade peripheral force was detailed to surround the house and its proximity, quietly preventing possible intruders from stumbling on the delicate, surgical operation. They were instructed to disengage one minute after the SWAT team was out of the building and in their vehicles.

Human and animal movement had been observed and studied for days in advance, day and night, to forewarn about any potential surprise.

Isaac read the document. He had read and written dozens of such documents in the course of his career. He felt that O, whom he had known well as a junior officer, had carried out a very professional and thorough preparation.

Reading O's words, he could almost smell the goat droppings and chicken dung on the basement floor, directly underneath the living room. Amazing, he thought, how Arab villagers could keep livestock in their smelly surroundings, sometimes just a few steps below shining marble floors, LCD screens and expensive Persian carpeting.

Vast differences lie between the two cultures, Arab and Jewish-Israeli, Isaac reflected.

O described a clean entry. His team, consisting of eight fighters, accessed the house by quietly forcing open the front door and three windows. There had been a head count of twenty-two persons, including women, children and adults, asleep in the house at the time of incursion. All were there. The room where the two brothers slept was reached within forty seconds of arrival at the front door. They were rifle butted out of bed and ordered to follow without argument. An expected amount of complaint was dealt with harshly, handcuffing the two behind their backs and blindfolding them. Everything was carried out in routine conformity with this type of action. One does not argue with a SWAT team making an arrest in the small hours of the night. Compliance with the team's demands isn't optional, or open to negotiation. The two alternatives are: come along willingly, or come along knocked out cold.

At the point when the apprehended brothers were being whisked through the living room towards the exit, all the other inhabitants were accounted for. Some awake, others asleep and all under watch. It was then that the father unexpectedly leaped forward and jumped on O. He grabbed the strap of the officer's M-16 short-version assault rifle, which O wore across his chest with enough strap slack for shouldering the weapon. The older man tried to strangle O by twisting the strap around his neck. As O began to choke, he reached for his handgun with his free hand. Tearing the pistol out of its secured thigh holster, he put the gun to the assaulting man's head and fired a single shot. The older man collapsed to the ground. O quickly instructed one of his men to shoulder lift and bring along the shot man. Then he proceeded to quietly command an otherwise clean exit. The whole violent event took seconds, and delayed the task force by very little. Other family members who had witnessed the horrifying incident were frozen in shock.

While the single gunshot reverberated, and the acrid smell of discharged weapon smoke was still in the air, O's team was already out of the house and inside their vehicles. They completed a quick but organised retreat, touching base two minutes later with the peripheral infantry force on the village outskirts.

The wounded man was transferred to an ambulance that awaited such an emergency. He was later proclaimed dead by the medical corps physician in the ambulance.

Isaac read the debriefing reports of O's team members as well. They were shorter and mostly corroborated their commander's report, adding or omitting a few facts, depending on the exact location of each member during the operation. Three of the reports were written by team members who had witnessed at close range the older man's unfortunate attempted assault, and the fatal shooting.

The next report in Yael's dossier was the medical summary from the ambulance crew. The physician reported that a forty-six-year-old man was brought into the ambulance at 2:06 a.m. suffering from extensive damage caused by a 9-mm gunshot wound on the left side of his cranium. There had been a massive loss of blood and no pulse. Due to the extensive cranial-vault derangement and lack of any vital signs, rescue procedures proved futile and were stopped after a few minutes. The person identified as Jamal Abdul-Rahman Toukan was pronounced dead.

There was another page signed by the emergency medical services of the Palestine Red Crescent Society in Hebron, confirming receipt of the corpse during the morning shift of February 3. It had been brought in by the UN and the Israeli military liaison officers in an Israeli Medical Corps ambulance. All medical reports were accompanied by photographs, for future forensic use.

The next two reports were written by the GSS interrogators who investigated both Ibrahim and Rafik Toukan. The expected arms and explosives stash was found in their house, but the interrogators were also led to a hiding place of ready-to-use suicide charges sewn into winter jackets. Their prospective operatives, two teenage Palestinians, were picked up and taken into custody. They had both been recruited by Rafik, but trained and instructed by other persons whom they had been introduced to at the mosque. Both boys were convinced that their reward was waiting in heaven in the form of pretty young virgins with alluring dark eyes. Money had been given as well, and more was promised for their impoverished families.

Obviously, the investigation had been thoroughly conducted, thought Isaac. It had become quite ramified, involving approximately a dozen arrests, based on information obtained from the two brothers, their teenage accomplices and several mosque-based instigators.

The last batch of papers involved correspondence with various civil rights and Palestinian welfare organisations. These were registered complaints and demands to bring to justice the officer who had shot and killed an unarmed older man at point-blank range. The fact that the SWAT team had forcibly broken into the family home in the small hours of the night was regarded as a serious "aggravating circumstance."

The suicide jackets and arms stash were completely ignored by these reports.

Senior command had ordered Lieutenant Colonel Yael Levy to study the case carefully and make a recommendation. Her input would have considerable weight at both levels: the military disciplinary court, and the army's interaction with the complaining foreign agencies, the latter pertaining to the UN or European Union organs involved with Palestinian welfare.

The particular paper trail that Isaac had read reflected high sensitivity. Yael's task had become an issue with significant implications, in the legal, foreign and public-relations realms.

Isaac wondered how, in such troubled times for the Hebron region, Norwegian, British or Dutch observers felt that they had a right to tell Israelis how to protect their civilian population and prevent definite terrorist mass-carnage attempts by suicide bombers in Jerusalem or Tel Aviv. But the military command's immediate concern now, Isaac assumed, would be to defuse this particular charge so that it would not be blown out of proportion. Avoiding an international media feast and saving the Israeli army from being held to blame for killing an innocent man – that was certainly high on the command's agenda.

The one-sidedness of European and UN observers, Isaac knew, would remain in the public's moral perception only until the incident blew over. Better prevent the media circus now rather than having to clear it up at great cost later, he thought. Having gone through the thick file, Isaac rang up Yael's office. Her driver came by and collected the material. Isaac arranged by telephone to meet Yael two days later.

Their meeting had been scheduled in her office, and she had requested Isaac's permission to turn on her tape recorder. That way, she claimed, they could converse freely without her having to take notes. Permission granted, Isaac approached the subject directly: "Fire away, what would you like to know?"

"Tell me your general impression of the times in question, the beginning of 2002. From an operational perspective, what governed your state of mind as you stood at the forefront of the anti-terror campaign?"

"We were living in the aftermath of two major influences at the time," answered Isaac. "The first influence was the Al-Aqsa Intifada – the Palestinian uprising of October 2000 following Chairman Arafat's rejection of Israel's peace offer by Prime Minister Barak. That event carried in its wake, among other operational tasks that we needed to deal with, a particularly bloody string of suicide attacks and other acts of unprovoked terror. It almost seemed that regardless of the negotiations, Arafat was intent on creating his own war of independence, no matter what.

"The second influence, of course, was September 11, 2001, and its backwash. Less than six months after 9/11, all nerve endings were bare and sensitive."

Yael absorbed his brief background summary. "I need to reason with O's action at the legal level. He had led a team of nine, including himself. These were highly trained, heavily armed fighters. He was in a civilian setup, not a military installation. No other firearms were in evidence other than those carried by his team. Nonetheless, when faced with some opposition, as a first choice he resorted to using his firearm, lethally wounding an unarmed older civilian. Under the circumstances and considering his training and capabilities, could he not deal with Toukan senior by unarmed combat, which we assume was part of his training? Why did he not at least make a first attempt at doing so before shooting? Perhaps even shoot to disable and halt the assault, stopping short of sentencing the man to certain death?"

Isaac barely paused to consider her question. "First and foremost, one must understand that a hostile person had grasped hold of O's weapon. This is by far the most dangerous operational problem, which no one can afford. The weapons in an operation such as the Beit Dahar one are loaded. They are carried with a chambered round and without a safety catch. That goes for the assault rifles as well as the handguns. Our men are trained to operate like this. The only safety catch in such an operation lies between the man's brain and his index finger." Isaac pointed his finger to his forehead, to emphasise this, and kept on.

"If the enemy gets close enough to touch your weapon during action, you obviously run the risk of uncontrolled discharge. This may endanger your teammates, innocent persons or yourself.

Operationally, a hostile person reaching for your gun cannot be tolerated. Anyone stupid enough to touch an assault-team member's gun is put down as quickly and as efficiently as possible. Toukan either made a terribly rash mistake of poor judgment, or a bad gamble. Either way, he paid an unfortunately high price. None of us particularly likes a messy operation. O acted on impulse. He was right to do so – in the tight spot that he was in there is room only for action, not for deliberation. Those are the rules of the game. That's how we're trained, and O complied 100 percent with his training. It's a lesson that both the enemy and we have learned the hard way."

He paused and added, "Moreover, any attempt to disrupt an operation of this nature must be stopped very forcefully. Otherwise, deterrence, as well as valuable time may be lost. Both are professional tools. Sometimes, an operation's success or failure may depend more on these assets than on sheer fighting skills."

Isaac waited a few seconds to let his words sink in before continuing. "In retrospect, O killed one person. Under the circumstances, the difference between success and disaster can be only a few seconds and one simple decision away. Had O gotten into a physical struggle with this fellow, no one could predict the extent of wasted time and operational compromise that the force might have suffered, thus endangering his team and the other innocent people within the house. We've had some bad experiences when relying on our physical ability to quickly overcome an opposing person. Surprisingly or not, some are very resilient. On a hair's breadth operation, a soldier's first fallback is the firearm. A nearly strangled person's immediate and justified reaction is resorting to his most trustworthy alternative. And O was being choked by the older man.

"Let me describe for you a perfectly feasible worst-case

scenario: Precious time is lost restraining the father in his attempt to halt his sons' arrest. The whole house is awake within a short time and more family members are drawn in, encouraged to follow a similar course of trying to resist the soldiers. To foil this and save their own lives, the task force may be compelled to fire at women and children. Some of the house's inhabitants might have time to reach the arms stash and discharge weapons or explosives. Neighbours may thus be alerted and the circle of violence expanded, throwing the infantry safeguarding force into action. What you could have on your hands now is an operation gone rancid. It could result in dozens of wounded or killed civilians and soldier casualties. A high probability of failure to secure and deliver the apprehended brothers, thus defeating the operation's purpose, is certainly an additional likely outcome. It may result in losing track of the suspect-terrorist network forever.

"At another level of hypothetical consideration, a military commission of inquiry easily fits into this equation of operational fiasco to give it an even livelier complexion. Also, consider the likelihood of an attack of this magnitude on a small village becoming an unnecessary international embarrassment.

"O's decision prevented all that prima facie, and at a minimal cost. That is what he was trained to do, and how he was taught to think and operate."

Yael swallowed hard and sipped some water. Isaac's harsh, matter-of-fact analysis was not easy to digest. She still found the situation in question hard to conceive of, even from a stance of academic distance. She had been around men such as Isaac for years, and now recognised that this was exactly the reason she requested Isaac's "rough and ready" input. Nonetheless, as close as she had been to their reality, Yael had never looked at a dangerous action situation straight in the eye. She had had only a secondhand understanding of how these men lived and felt as soldiers.

Deep under the professional respect, sympathy, comradeship and even love that she had felt towards these men for years, there had also been fear. Not personal fear of any one of them as an individual killer – never once in her whole career had she felt even a hint of a threat. These men seemed to have erected a thick concrete wall between their operational skills and their personal lives. Her fear evolved from an abstract feeling generated by the swift, phenomenal change in their personality. When push came to shove, they would instantly become cold, metallic, lethal killing machines. She had lived, worked, laughed, mingled and identified with men capable not only of taking life at the drop of a hat, but also of carrying on afterwards as if nothing had happened.

"I think that I understand the operational constraints better now," said Yael. "But my duty in this case as military court judge revolves around one crucial question: Can O's action be defined as that of a 'reasonable person'? This is actually a legal term and not a casual description. Would a 'reasonable person' have acted in the way that O had chosen to act? If the answer is yes, then my recommendation may be to justify his conduct. Otherwise, disciplinarian measures, or charges leading to a court-martial are likely to be implemented."

Isaac's brow furrowed as he took a moment to reflect. "You say 'reasonable person'?" he asked, inflecting the words slowly to emphasise their weight. Yael nodded.

"Tell me, what reasonable person goes out at 2:00 a.m. on a cold February night, wearing a twelve-kilo ceramic bulletproof vest, two loaded firearms, a gun belt and a communications set? Thus outfitted, he sets out to enter a hostile house known to have hidden arms and explosives in a hostile village, teeming with terror activists.

"What reasonable man spends years in intensive training and subsequently makes a career of apprehending suicide killers hiding in dark airless crypts and mosque basements? What is reasonable about a man who may lie in a sewer for three days, stalking a lurking terrorist?

"Our reality does not even begin to conform to your definition of a reasonable person. He does not reflect in our mirror, and only exists in legal textbooks designed to make the lives of judges and prosecutors fit into a paradigm that you can live with. But we cannot. We have a job to do. If we fail to do it, thirty innocent, real 'reasonable persons' may be blown up tomorrow in a city bus, a restaurant or a supermarket. O's conduct cannot be evaluated and assessed with your terminology, based on an abstract, imaginary reasonable person. He is an anti-terror fighter, not a reasonable person.

"His life story may not suggest itself at first sight, but it is not an atypical one for our force. Basically, O is a fine lad. After his compulsory service in the parachute brigade, he studied mathematics at the university. He had finished his degree with distinction when one of SWAT's commanders, who knew him, took the trouble to go to his campus and persuaded him to re-enlist. He later even half-completed a master's degree in operational analysis while serving as a career officer in SWAT.

"O operated with the sharp precision and accuracy of a Swiss army knife. His judgment was clear, efficient and faultless. Unlike a murderer, he lacks criminal tendency. But like most of us, he is a trained professional soldier who performed his job to the best of his ability. This is how he was taught to act and what he is best at. Now, go ahead and tell me if he passed your 'reasonable person' test."

The Maths Teacher
2009

By the time he turned forty-five, Jason Markowitz had undergone a triple bypass heart surgery and two lumbar-disc operations. Modern health care and his good fortune saved him from disability and an early grave; medicine afforded a new lease on his life following orthopaedic and preventive cardiologic interventions. Nonetheless, he had been given serious warning. The Almighty had apparently decided that He wasn't finished with Jason and provided him with an additional path out of harm's way.

Jason had devoted nearly two decades to the foundation and development of an extremely successful communications software company. He had paid with nearly twenty years of working an outrageous amount of hours a day in the competitive, cut-throat elite programmer's market. Stressful workloads, too much coffee and too many cigarettes had taken a heavy toll on his health. This lifestyle only added insult to the injury caused by an inherited weak heart. Fortunately, he had been able to bale out in time. A major national telephone company bought his business lock, stock and software. After splitting the goings with his two associates and the taxman, he was still left with about five million dollars in liquid assets. Jason decided to cash in, retire early and look after his failing health as a first priority. Thus he pensioned himself off at the age of forty-five following his doctors' advice. He took up bicycling and trekking, made an attempt at eating healthy and reduced his smoking quota to five cigarettes a week.

After two years of leading a healthy, non-stressful existence Jason began to feel bored. He couldn't bear the idea that his mind would be entertained until doomsday solely with planning the next bike course or mountain trek. At that point he decided to go back to university and take up mathematics. Twenty years before he had earned a master's degree in computer engineering from MIT, but mathematics had been his first love. Only the dubious practicality of a maths degree had directed him towards computer science and software. But now he could afford to study mathematics for its own sake to his heart's content. Jason therefore enrolled in a challenging Ivy League BSc maths programme and graduated with distinction four years later. He was proud of having bright twenty-year-old classmates and worked as hard for his achievement as this post-pubescent crowd.

Upon graduating, he felt like putting his skill to good use for a worthy cause. Pondering how to go about this, he thought of embarking on a self-inflicted crusade as a high school maths teacher. The rationale behind his yearning to teach school maths was based on the sad but well-founded assumption that there was a great shortage of good teachers in this field. Many intelligent pupils find maths unassailable due to inadequate teaching methods. Jason had recognised this problem while still in school, since many of his peers suffered its consequences. He felt that his purpose in life now was to change this trend and decipher maths at all levels through creative didactics.

Almost every Friday afternoon, Jason met for lunch with Kevin and Ron, his two ex-associates. These were trusted old friends who had stayed in the software business. He shared his new idea with them.

"Have you ever taught? I mean, stood in front of a class?" Kevin asked. Jason replied that he hadn't. Smiling benevolently, Kevin, who had taught high school for a couple of years, said to him, "In that case, on your first day as a teacher you may find that while your aim is to be the saviour of education on planet Earth, you end up being a glorified babysitter for adolescents, the majority of whom are bored and uninterested in studying. They are generally hyperhormonal and abusive of geriatric cases aged thirty plus who dare stand in front of them. But do not be deterred, brother. Go ahead, dive in at the deep end and enjoy teaching."

Jason obtained part-time employment teaching ninth-grade maths for six hours a week in a public school. The school was understaffed and the principal was in desperate need of a maths teacher. She was impressed with Jason's track record and understood his motivation for taking the job. Yet she considered him overqualified. "You don't need to have a maths degree with distinction from a fancy university to teach ninth-grade algebra in my school."

Jason appreciated her candour but chose to ignore her warning.

On his first day at work, he sat in the faculty room realising that most of the teaching staff were in their early thirties, twenty years his juniors. Even the principal was only forty-one. But Jason felt that he was a man with a mission, determined to integrate into the teaching world. He noticed that his image of a retired, affluent hi-tech maverick would prove inadequate and therefore exchanged it for a more acceptable one. He started wearing denims, shaved his chin only twice a week and bicycled to school. This camouflage broke the ice between Jason and other staff, and also made him more approachable to his pupils. He was teaching maths to ninth-grade kids and life seemed perfect, at least for a while.

Trouble began a few months later, when one evening Jason received a telephone call.

"Hello, Mr. Markowitz. This is Jennifer Garcia. I'm Laurie Garcia's mother."

"Good evening, Mrs. Garcia. How can I help you?"

"My daughter is in your maths class, and you gave her zero on an assignment that she handed in late."

"To be accurate, Mrs. Garcia, I did grade her zero, but for work that she didn't hand in at all. I had no other choice, as all the rest of her class did meet the deadline and completed their work on time."

"But she asked to hand in her homework just a few days late. Surely you could accept that?"

"In all truth I would have, had she called me in advance and told me that she had a problem and needed a few more days. This happens sometimes. But Laurie simply didn't do her work and expected me to accept it when she was good and ready. That's different."

"I don't see what difference it makes. After all, you are perfectly able to grade her work even a few days after you have graded the others."

"I appreciate your honest attempt to arrange my tasking schedule, but the point is that I expect my pupils to be serious and responsible about their duties. For instance, one of the girls in her class was sick, yet had the presence of mind to ask a friend to come by her home and pick up her work so that she could meet the deadline. Laurie ignored all this and that's the reason for the grade."

"Aren't you supposed to teach maths? What's all this about 'duty'?"

"I'm talking about education, Mrs. Garcia. Not only maths. I value punctuality and responsibility no less than mathematics."

"But you're ruining her GPA! She needs a grade point average of at least 75 to get into college."

"She has plenty of opportunities to make up for it in the future provided that she hands in all her homework on time. Good evening to you, Mrs. Garcia."

The following day Jason was summoned from the staff room to the principal's office. Although she fully supported his stance over Laurie Garcia, the principal tried to convince him to make an exception.

"Look, Jason, I have a whole issue on my hands now with Mrs. Garcia claiming that you discriminate against Hispanic pupils. She spoke to some other parents and is trying to provoke a mini-Latino revolt."

Jason scratched the stubble on his chin. "Mrs. Garcia shouldn't get too far with that tactic. My star pupil is Ed Contreras with a 100 average score and an A+. I also awarded Ana María Saucedo five bonus points. She had the presence of mind to give a classmate her homework before the deadline, despite having stayed at home with a fever. I'm simply trying to mould responsible human beings out of your freshmen, instead of just algebra-equation automatons."

Thus Jason stood his ground and refused to accept Laurie's late assignment. Although his class generally did well in maths and their end-of-year achievement was well above the school's average, Jason's contract was not renewed. The Garcia incident had recurred during the school year in several variations. The PTA (Parent-Teacher Association) had recognised his qualities as a maths teacher but voted for his dismissal. The principal had little choice but to tell him that she could not offer him a teaching post for the coming year.

Kevin and Ron had listened to the full account over their Friday lunchtime meetings. Kevin had thought that the experience would wean Jason of his pedagogical venture and bring him back to the sad reality. But Jason's appetite had just been tickled. He somewhat bitterly decided that the teaching appointment that he had failed to retain fell short of his true capability. He now sought a quality teaching post.

Located in the heart of upper-middle-class suburbia, the expensive private school that Jason next interviewed at fitted his natural milieu perfectly. Ron, who had gone to college with the principal, spoke to him and recommended Jason. This time, he arrived at the interview in a three-piece suit and felt awful about it. Somewhat conscious of his background, he did not wish to become a snob or be associated with their like. The principal, a man his age, had already told him on the phone that he was looking for a high-calibre maths teacher who would prepare his juniors and seniors interested in calculus and trigonometry for maths ACT tests. This setup seemed to fit Jason's profile better. He felt that an elite maths class with motivated students was more up his street than the public school crowd that he had tried and failed to mould according to his standards.

The principal, who had graduated from Syracuse University in New York, was most impressed with Jason's master's degree in computer science from MIT and cum laude in mathematics from Columbia. Jason began teaching at his school the following week, but retained the denim and stubble which he found comfortable. While his appearance caused no incident, his approach to mathematics did. After a few weeks of working with his students, complaints started streaming into the principal's office.

"Mr. Markowitz, some of your students and their parents have called my attention to your teaching methods. They are concerned about your ability to prepare the class for their ACT tests."

"I'm aware of some dissent regarding my way of teaching. But there is only one way to learn maths – that is to understand it. Many of my students have a poor understanding of the basis of mathematics and mathematical thinking. They are bright young people, misled for years. They were taught ways to bypass fundamental concepts. Instead of fearless sailing through the labyrinth of school mathematics, these youngsters were taught shortcuts to comprehension. Instead of sound logic, they were fed formulae-based problem-solving techniques. Yet maths is both; it is a maze but at the same time, a logical construction built brick by brick and layer on layer. Maths should be unraveled and not eschewed."

The principal considered this declaration.

"Most of your audience thinks that valuable time is being wasted on learning abstruse principles at the expense of problem solving, and especially, of practicing exam questions from previous years. Other schools do this for hours every day ad nauseam, believing that practice makes perfect."

"I don't quite think so. I'm trying to get many of the students to unlearn bad habits and think maths effectively. Once this is accomplished, the road will be paved to solving any exercise, including last year's exam. This is my way to make practice perfect. I aim for gold!"

While the principal thought that Jason aimed for the "gold medal" using the Olympic Games' metaphor, the teacher of course meant the "golden mean" of the Fibonacci series...

The principal, who understood little about maths, couldn't argue with Jason's rationale. On the other hand, he couldn't afford to take a chance with his seniors who would in a few short months need to tackle exam papers crucial to their future. Since he had the means, he hired a second maths teacher to work with the graduating class on exam questions, leaving Jason to his idiosyncratic teaching methods. When Jason found out about this he confronted the principal, telling him that a train engine could not have two drivers at the same time. Yet neither the student body nor their parents wished to abandon the idea of adding extra time for practicing exam questions. The class did well on their ACT exams and Jason was given full credit for their success. Nevertheless, he chose to resign from his post. The school regretted this but did not insist on his staying.

After going through the Sisyphean task of starting all over in a few more schools, Jason found that he could retain his appointments no longer than two or three semesters. Invariably, showdown time arrived when he graded mediocre students with Cs and Ds and had to confront their GPA-conscious parents. Another recurring hurdle concerned Jason's schedule. He couldn't put up with inefficient schedule management and continually quarreled with the secretary and principal. Although highly regarded by senior teaching supervisors, he couldn't hold a teaching job. He only found solace when working with a maths-club class initiated by his alma mater to cater for those interested in maths for its own sake. This group of youngsters, mostly but not solely from high schools, met with Jason in class on the Columbia University campus for three hours a week. They had no need to pass exams and were there for the love of it.

Kevin and Ron listened to Jason's misgivings one Friday afternoon. He complained bitterly. "Intelligent fourteen year olds known to have an IQ of 120 or higher were given a simple test that I devised for high school freshmen. They were all aware since age five that $1+1=2$. That was my prerequisite and they all complied 100 percent. But seven out of ten could not solve the simple question, $a+a=?$ The majority did not know that the correct answer was $2a$, nor did it seem to be their obvious choice. This reflects a basic teaching flaw. Yet most of them turned down an opportunity to learn basic algebra from scratch and opted for solving a hundred exam questions instead. Now that's doing things the hard way, and it means that in all likelihood there will be severe gaps in their understanding of conceptual maths."

Ron listened patiently to Jason's rant. "You can't expect to become a white knight who rides into the educational system on a stallion and saves the day in one fell swoop. The picture you reflect is rather that of a pathetic, grouchy, middle-aged man trying to put the world right. Your complaints are as bad as Hamlet's: *'The time is out of joint; O cursed spite. That ever I was born to set it right.'*

"Stay with the maths club at Columbia University. That best fits both your capabilities and temper."

A few weeks later, Ron was stuck with one of his projects and called Jason for some advice. They met at Ron's office and decided that Jason would take over and try to find a systematic solution. It took him twenty-four hours to learn the updated information required to work the riddle, and three days to solve the problem. A week later, he had the programme neatly tied up and packaged. They met again and Ron, having studied the package, was amazed by the simple elegance of Jason's solution.

"You're still the best. I don't understand why you ever bother to grapple with high school maths and the inherent mediocrity of our education system."

Jason thought about Ron's assertion and replied, "That's exactly the reason why I wanted to teach maths. I feel that this way I can make a difference and leave a mark on the world of mathematics. Helping you out is fine. But a new computer programme today gets washed away like wet sand on the ocean's waterline tomorrow. By next year no one will even remember what it was for. That's not my idea of an aim in life."

"Jason, you don't even begin to fathom how wrong you are. The Information Security software package that you wrote when you recruited Kevin and me twenty-eight years ago, for example, worked well and was only replaced three years ago, surviving generations of hardware and serving its purpose for a quarter of a century. You already are a legend and even today, almost ten years after your retirement, much of my business still rides on the waves generated by your reputation. You are probably one of the best software experts turned out by the industry. You must accept that you will never be a mathematician of Einstein's, or Russell's calibre – but you are one of this world's computer science outstanding few. We have no knowledge of how this attribute may retain the name Jason Markowitz in the 'genius hall of fame.' That truly depends on the eternal fluidity of cyber science. But don't belittle this achievement or underrate what you can still contribute. Instead, focus on what you can do better than most other human beings. Just learn to enjoy it."

He picked up Jason's recent software solution from his desk and waved it as proof. Handing Jason a company cheque for $45,000, he commented that Jason's contribution to the project was worth ten times that.

Ron wanted Jason to make a partial comeback into the hi-tech industry and serve as his special consultant and troubleshooter. Frustrated with teaching maths, Jason reflected on Ron's theorem and decided to put Ron's request on a ninety-day trial term. He took up whatever projects Ron found that he could contribute towards and built a working schedule.

At first, Jason felt that he had completed a full circle, finally finding peace of mind in doing what he was best able to do. He retained his appointment with the university maths club but showed up at Ron's office whenever he wanted to work. He realised that Ron's plan needed to be put to the test of practice and tried to "go with the flow" and evaluate the situation as he went along.

Three months later, the trio met for lunch at one of their

favourite Friday watering holes. Jason announced that although he would always be prepared to come in and give Ron a hand, he wasn't willing to make a comeback and keep to it.

"To do this kind of work, one needs to be both razor sharp and hungry. One is contingent upon the other and I'm neither. Getting software out of trouble a few months ago by making a ten-day concentrated effort is fine. However, taking responsibility over a projected quarterly work graph gave me an important insight. It landed me back in square one and I have no wish to be there. I managed to extricate myself by the skin of my teeth from where it had almost killed me nearly ten years ago. I found that with this comeback my working hours progressively increased every week, as did the number of the coffee cups I drank and my blood pressure. I'm back to smoking every day and that's no good.

"I can't cope with stressful work and I certainly don't need the money. Since my retirement, I have barely scratched the surface of my capital. I lead a fairly frugal lifestyle, spending money mostly on bicycle trips and walking treks abroad once a year. My broker has cleverly invested in solid successful ventures. He steered clear of Bernard Madoff's Ponzi schemes, and even the 2008 meltdown didn't make much of a dent in my portfolio. But I want my life back without worrying about Ron's projects."

Ron had to accept this without argument. He was truly concerned about what Jason said regarding stress, cigarettes and blood pressure. Now he wished that he hadn't called Jason back from the cold to come and help him.

Kevin had listened to the whole exchange without saying much. Once they had moved on to other topics of conversation he quietly asked him, "Well, what will you do now that you have time on your hands again?"

Jason thought for a while, seemed lost for words and finally said unconvincingly, "I guess that I'll focus on my aficionado mathematicians in the pre-university club at Columbia. Even if just two or three of them choose maths as their major, I will have fulfilled my quest."

.ingramcontent.com/pod-product-compliance
ng Source LLC
burg PA
53040426
0014B/2395